THE ALMIGHTY SOMETIMES

by Kendall Feaver

The first performance of
THE ALMIGHTY SOMETIMES
was at the Royal Exchange Theatre
on 9 February 2018

THE ALMIGHTY SOMETIMES
By Kendall Feaver

Cast

ANNA	**Norah Lopez Holden**
RENEE	**Julie Hesmondhalgh**
OLIVER	**Mike Noble**
VIVIENNE	**Sharon Duncan-Brewster**

Creative Team

Director	Katy Rudd
Designer	Rosanna Vize
Lighting	Lucy Carter
Sound	Giles Thomas
Movement	Vicki Manderson
Assistant Director	Atri Banerjee
Casting Directors	Jerry Knight-Smith CDG and Vicky Richardson

Stage Manager	Harriet Stewart
Deputy Stage Manager	Leona Nally
Assistant Stage Manager	Amber Chapell

CAST

SHARON DUNCAN-BREWSTER (Vivienne) previously performed at the Royal Exchange Theatre in A STREETCAR NAME DESIRE (for which she won the UK Theatre Best Supporting Performance Award), SO SPECIAL and recently at the Bruntwood Prize Ceremony 2017. Other theatre credits include: VICTORY CONDITION, NUCLEAR WAR, HOPE, BABIES (Royal Court Jerwood Theatre); MEET ME AT DAWN, SWALLOW (Traverse Theatre); TRADE, A SEASON IN THE CONGO (Young Vic Theatre); THE IPHIGENIA QUARTET, YERMA (Gate Theatre); A MIDSUMMER NIGHT'S DREAM (Liverpool Everyman); A FEW MAN FRIDAYS (Cardboard Citizens); THE SWAN, THERE IS A WAR (National Theatre); LET THERE BE LOVE, BLUES FOR MR CHARLIE, FABULATION, PLAYBOY OF THE WEST INDIES, THE BLACK AND WHITE SEASON (Tricycle Theatre); THE HORSE MARINES (Theatre Royal Plymouth); THE BACCHAE (National Theatre of Scotland/Lyric Hammersmith/Lincoln Center, New York); BLACK CROWS (Clean Break/Arcola Theatre); GADDAFI (English National Opera); DIRTY BUTTERFLY (Soho Theatre); PEEPSHOW (Frantic Assembly); CRAVE (Paines Plough/Traverse Theatre/Royal Court/Berlin Sophiensaele); YARD GAL (Clean Break/Royal Court/MCC New York) and THE NO BOYS CRICKET CLUB (Theatre Royal Stratford East). Television credits include: TOP BOY; THE MIMIC; THE BIBLE (3 roles which won Sharon the Screen Nation Best Female Performance in TV Award 2014); DOCTOR WHO; CUCUMBER; EASTENDERS; BAD GIRLS; HOLBY CITY; SHOOT THE MESSENGER; CUFFS, DOCTORS; WAKING THE DEAD; BABY FATHER; CASUALTY; THE BILL; THE JOURNEY: EA Sports FIFA 17/18 videogame drama. Film credits include: STAR WARS: ROGUE ONE and THREE AND OUT. Short film credits include: CLASS 15; BLUES FOR NIA and MOCKINGBIRD.

JULIE HESMONDHALGH (Renee) trained at LAMDA and has previously performed at the Royal Exchange Theatre in THE GREATEST PLAY IN THE HISTORY OF THE WORLD, WIT (Manchester Theatre Award, Best Female Performance), BLACK ROSES: THE KILLING OF SOPHIE LANCASTER (MTA, Best Studio Performance), BLINDSIDED, the BRUNTWOOD PRIZE CEREMONY 2015 and MUCH ADO ABOUT NOTHING. Other theatre includes: THE REPORT with Lemn Sissay, GOD BLESS

THE CHILD (Royal Court). Television credits include: BROADCHURCH 3, HAPPY VALLEY 2, INSIDE NO 9: LA COUCHETTE, BLACK ROSES (RTS NW Award, Best Actor), MOVING ON, CUCUMBER, CORONATION STREET (series regular 1997–2013). Film credits include: PETERLOO, POND LIFE. She is co-founder of Manchester theatre collective TAKE BACK.

NORAH LOPEZ HOLDEN (Anna) has previously worked on OUR TOWN for the Royal Exchange Theatre. Other theatre credits include: OTHELLO (The Tobacco Factory); GHOSTS (HOME Manchester); EPIC LOVE AND POP SONGS (Pleasance Dome). Radio credits include: FBI'S MOST WANTED WOMAN: ASSATA SHAKUR (BBC Radio 4).

MIKE NOBLE (Oliver) has previously worked on PUNK ROCK for the Royal Exchange Theatre, which then transferred to Lyric Hammersmith. Other theatre credits include: ROAD, BAD ROADS (Royal Court Theatre); GAME (Almeida Theatre); THE CURIOUS INCIDENT OF THE DOG IN THE NIGHT TIME, PORT (National Theatre); MUDLARKS (Hightide Festival/Bush Theatre). Television credits include: HOME FIRES 1 and 2; MR SELFRIDGE 3; GRANTCHESTER; PRISONER'S WIVES. Film credits include: DARK RIVER; THE SIEGE OF JADOTVILLE; BACHELOR GAMES; KILL COMMAND; JACK RYAN: SHADOW; JADOO; PRIVATE PEACEFUL; WORLD WAR Z; GAMBIT.

CREATIVE TEAM

KENDALL FEAVER (Writer) won the Judges Award at the 2015 Bruntwood Prize for Playwriting for her play, THE ALMIGHTY SOMETIMES. After the Royal Exchange, a second production will follow at Griffin Theatre Company, Sydney. Kendall graduated with a Masters in Writing for Performance from Goldsmiths University, supported by the Ian Potter Cultural Trust Award. She has been on attachment at the National Theatre Studio and is developing an original musical as part of the National Theatre's Musical Theatre Group. THE ALMIGHTY SOMETIMES is Kendall's first professional production.

KATY RUDD (Director) makes her debut at the Royal Exchange as Director. Katy brings a breadth of directing experience having previously worked as an Associate Director on HUSBANDS & SONS in 2016 (National Theatre/Royal Exchange Theatre) and in 2017 on GROUNDHOG DAY (Old Vic and Broadway) and PINOCCHIO (National Theatre). Prior to this she was part of the team behind THE CURIOUS INCIDENT OF THE DOG IN THE NIGHT-TIME (National Theatre, West End, Broadway and UK Tour) working as Associate Director from the show's inception and directing the show for its reopening at the Gielgud Theatre and for the UK tour. Katy began her career at the Salisbury Playhouse as winner of the Noël Coward Young Director's Bursary, and in 2011 she was appointed staff director at the National Theatre. Other credits as an Associate Director include THE TWITS and LINDA (Royal Court), THE MASTER BUILDER (Old Vic) and MOJO (West End).

ROSANNA VIZE (Designer) trained at Bristol Old Vic Theatre School. She has worked regularly as an assistant to Anna Fleischle and was the resident design assistant for the RSC from September 2014 to September 2015. She was a Linbury Prize Finalist in 2013 working with English Touring Opera and is currently one of the Jerwood Young Designers. Theatre includes: YOUS TWO, NO ONE WILL TELL ME HOW TO START A REVOLUTION (Hampstead Theatre); KING LEAR (Globe Theatre); EARTHWORKS, MYTH (RSC); LOW LEVEL PANIC (Orange Tree Theatre); AFTER OCTOBER (Finborough Theatre); HENRY I (Reading Between the Lines); GIRLS (Soho Theatre, Hightide and Talawa Theatre); FUP (Kneehigh Theatre); NOYE'S FLUDDE (Kneehigh Theatre); DARK LAND LIGHTHOUSE (Bristol Old Vic); ST JOAN OF THE STOCKYARDS (Bristol Old Vic); A THOUSAND SEASONS PASSED, THE TINDER BOX, THE LAST DAYS OF MANKIND and TALON (Bristol Old Vic); DIARY OF A MADMAN and THE RISE AND SHINE OF COMRADE FIASCO (Gate Theatre); INFINITE LIVES, COASTAL DEFENCES (Tobacco Factory Theatre); BANKSY: THE ROOM IN THE ELEPHANT, (Tobacco Factory Theatre and Traverse Theatre); EDWARD GANTS AMAZING FEATS OF LONELINESS, THE WICKED LADY (Bristol Old Vic Theatre School); THE PICTURE OF JOHN GREY (The Old Red

Lion); MEASURE FOR MEASURE (Oxford School of Drama). Opera includes: EUGENE ONEGIN (Arcola Theatre); DON GIOVANNI (Hampstead Garden Opera); A MIDSUMMER NIGHT'S DREAM (RSC and Garsington Opera).

LUCY CARTER (Lighting Designer) has previously worked on PERSUASION and HUSBANDS AND SONS (which went on to National Theatre) for the Royal Exchange Theatre. Lucy is a two-time winner of the Knight of Illumination Award for WOOLF WORKS and CHROMA; winner of the 2013 TMA Achievement award in Opera for LOHENGRIN; and the 2004 Olivier Dance Award for 2 HUMAN. Lighting Designer credits include: ELEKTRA (Goteborg Opera, Sweden); THE DREAM OF GERONTIUS (English National Opera at The Royal Festival Hall); LOHENGRIN (Greek National Opera, Athens); +− HUMAN (Roundhouse); AUTOBIOGRAPHY (Sadler's Wells); INFRA (Royal Danish Ballet); GENUS (National Ballet Canada); EVERYBODY'S TALKING ABOUT JAMIE (Apollo); WOOLF WORKS, MULTIVERSE, CARBON LIFE − revival (Royal Ballet); OIL (Almeida); LA NUIT S'ACHEVE (Mariinsky Theatre Gala); APPASIONATA (Pacific Northwest Ballet); DYAD 1929 (Houston Ballet); THE END OF LONGING, starring Matthew Perry (ATG Productions Ltd).

GILES THOMAS (Sound Designer) has previously worked for the Royal Exchange Theatre on HOW MY LIGHT IN SPENT, WISH LIST, YEN (also Royal Court); POMONA (also Orange Tree, National Theatre, Offie Nomination, Best Sound Designer). Composition and sound design credits include: THE IMPORTANCE OF BEING EARNEST (UK tour); WAIT UNTIL DARK (UK tour); HANDBAGGED (Theatre by the Lake); DEATH OF A SALESMAN (Royal & Derngate); OTHELLO (Tobacco Factory, Bristol); CONTRACTIONS (Sheffield Theatres); CORRESPONDENCE (Old Red Lion); I SEE YOU, WOLF FROM THE DOOR, PRIME TIME, MINT, PIGEONS, DEATH TAX and THE PRESIDENT HAS COME TO SEE YOU (Royal Court); SPARKS (Old Red Lion); THE TITANIC ORCHESTRA, THIS WILL END BADLY, ALLIE (Edinburgh); LITTLE MALCOLM AND HIS STRUGGLE AGAINST THE EUNUCHS (Southwark Playhouse); OUTSIDE MULLINGAR (Theatre Royal Bath); BACK DOWN (Birmingham Rep); LIE WITH ME (Talawa); THE SOUND OF YELLOW (Young Vic); TAKE A DEEP BREATH AND BREATHE and THE STREET (Oval House Theatre). Sound design credits include: HIJABI MONOLOGUES (Bush Theatre); DISCO PIGS (Trafalgar Studios and Irish Rep NY); THE UGLY ONE, A DARK NIGHT IN DALSTON (Park Theatre); WHAT SHADOWS (Birmingham Rep); THEY DRINK IT IN THE CONGO (Almeida); THE SUGAR-COATED BULLETS OF THE BOURGEOISIE (Arcola, HighTide Festival); ORSON'S SHADOW, SUPERIOR DONUTS (Southwark Playhouse); BETRAYAL (UK tour); THE SNOW QUEEN (Nuffield and Royal & Derngate); A HARLEM DREAM (Young Vic); KHANDAN (Birmingham Repand Royal Court); THREE MEN IN A BOAT (UK tour); KING JOHN (Union); IT'S ABOUT TIME (nabakov) and SHOOT/GET TREASURE/REPEAT (Out of Joint).

VICKI MANDERSON (Movement Director). Her previous credits include: COCKPIT (Lyceum Edinburgh); WE'RE STILL HERE (National Theatre Wales); JIMMY'S HALL (Abbey Theatre); 306 (National Theatre of Scotland); A PROFOUNDLY AFFECTIONATE, PASSIONATE DEVOTION TO SOMEONE – NOUN (Royal Court); SEE ME NOW (Young Vic); THE TEMPEST (Beijing Xinchan); DETAILS (Grid Iron); KIDNAPPED (RCS); HOUSED (Old Vic New Voices); A SERIOUS CASE OF THE FUCKITS, LOADED, I DO BELIEVE IN MONSTERS, LOADED (Royal Central School of Speech and Drama). Associate Movement Director credits include: THE TWITS (Royal Court); LET THE RIGHT ONE IN (National Theatre of Scotland/Royal Court/West End); THE CURIOUS INCIDENT OF THE DOG IN THE NIGHT-TIME (National Theatre/West End); BLACKWATCH, IN TIME OF STRIFE (National Theatre Scotland).

ATRI BANERJEE (Assistant Director) is Trainee Director at the Royal Exchange Theatre as part of his Theatre Directing MFA at Birkbeck, University of London. Atri's directing credits include: THE COMEDY OF ERRORS (Japan and UK tour); SIX CHARACTERS IN SEARCH OF AN AUTHOR (C Venues, Edinburgh Festival Fringe and ADC); BIG MAC (Sweet ECA, Edinburgh Festival Fringe); CAMBRIDGE FOOTLIGHTS SPRING REVUE: THE HISTORY OF EVERYTHING and AIDA (ADC); ACCIDENTAL DEATH OF AN ANARCHIST and THE LAST FIVE YEARS (Corpus Playroom). Associate Director credits include: JUBILEE (Royal Exchange Theatre and Lyric Hammersmith). Assisting credits include: OUR TOWN (Royal Exchange Theatre), HENRY V (Cambridge Arts Theatre), DIDO, QUEEN OF CARTHAGE (Emmanuel College Chapel and Senate House, Cambridge). Writing credits include: SIX CHARACTERS IN SEARCH OF AN AUTHOR (adaptation) and BIG MAC (as co-writer). Atri is a member of the Tamasha Developing Artists network and of Artistic Directors of the Future.

Australian Government

This project has been assisted by the Australian Government through the Australia Council, its arts funding and advisory body

Manchester's Royal Exchange Theatre Company transforms the way people see theatre, each other and the world around them.

Their historic building, once the world's biggest cotton exchange, was taken over by artists in 1976. Today it is an award-winning cultural charity that produces new theatre in-the-round, in communities, on the road and online.

The Exchange's unique auditorium is powerfully democratic, a space where audiences and performers meet as equals, entering and exiting through the same doors. It is the inspiration for all they do; inviting everyone to understand the past, engage in today's big questions, collectively imagine a better future and lose themselves in the moment of a great night out.

The Royal Exchange is currently nominated for both Regional Theatre of the Year and School of the Year at *The Stage* Awards 2018. The Spring–Summer Season features work from an incredible array of artists from across Manchester and beyond. It includes new adaptations of Mary Shelley's FRANKENSTEIN by April De Angelis, and Chekhov's THE CHERRY ORCHARD translated by Rory Mullarkey; a new play by Associate Artist Maxine Peake, QUEENS OF THE COAL AGE, alongside her return to the stage to play Winnie in Samuel Beckett's HAPPY DAYS. Associate Artists RashDash and new partners Yellow Earth bring their distinctive performance styles to The Studio.

Find out more at **royalexchange.co.uk**

instagram.com/rxtheatre

facebook.com/rxtheatre

youtube.com/royalexchange.co.uk

Registered Charity Number 255424

ROYAL EXCHANGE STAFF LIST

Director of Creative Learning **Inga Hirst**
Producer (Creative Learning and Engagement) **Chris Wright**
Elders Programme Leader **Andy Barry**
Young People's Programme Leader **Matt Hassall**
Schools Programme Leader **Chelsea Morgan**
Youth Engagement Programme Leader (Outreach) **Parvez Qadir**
Community Programme Leader **Tracie Daly**
Administrator **Emma Wallace**

DEVELOPMENT

Development Director **Val Young**
Senior Development Manager **Gina Fletcher**
Individual Giving Manager **Becky Rosenthal**
Corporate Development Manager **Christina Georgiou**
Development Executive **Holli Leah**
Development Assistant **Melissa Brakel**

DIRECTORATE

Executive Director **Mark Dobson**
Artistic Director **Sarah Frankcom**
Associate Artistic Directors **Amit Sharma, Matthew Xia**
Associate Artists **Amanda Dalton, Rash Dash, Chris Goode, Imogen Knight, Maxine Peake, Benji Reid, Chris Thorpe, Don Warrington**
Assistant to the Artistic Directorate & Executive Director **Michelle Hickman**
Birkbeck Trainee Director **Atri Banerjee**
RTYDS Resident Assistant Director **Nickie Miles-Wildin**

ELDERS COMPANY

Alan Maguire, Amina Latimer, Anne Tober, Anthony Joyce, Brenda Hickey, Charles McDermott, Christine Connor, Christopher Littler, David Weston, Donald McGregor, Doreen Robinson, Dudley Newell, Estelle Longmore, Glyn Treharne, Gordon Emerson, Graham Gillis, Jacquie Long, Janice Bonner, Jean Wood, Judith Wood, Kenneth Walker, Liz Aniteye, Marianne Downes, Maureen Stirpe, Michael Williams, Monica Farry, Pauline Sergeant, Pete Shotton, Peter Jones, Philip Haynes, Sandy Parkinson, Shelia Colman, Steve Stubbs, Tony Cocker, Val Collier

FINANCE & ADMINISTRATION

Director of Finance & Administration **Barry James**
HR Manager (Maternity Cover) **Sara Spencer**
Finance Manager (interim) Gurjinder Kang
Orders & Purchase Ledger Clerk **Jennifer Ellis**
Payroll Clerk **Carl Robson**
Finance Administrator **Elizabeth Coupe**

GREEN ROOM

Supervisor **Yvonne Stott**
Assistant **Anne Dardis**

MARKETING

Director of Marketing & Communications (Maternity Cover) **Laura Arends**
Head of Marketing **Vanessa Walters**
Communications Manager **Paula Rabbitt**
Marketing Officer – Groups, Education & Development **Eleanor Higgins**
Marketing Officer – Digital and Systems **Vicky Wormald**
Marketing Officer **Anneka Morley**
Marketing Assistant **Justina Aina**
Digital Marketing Officer **Ashley McKay**
Box Office Manager **Sue Partington**
Box Office Assistants **William Barnett, Jon Brennan, Lindsay Burke, Tracey Fleet, Dan Glynn, Zoe Nicholas, Christine Simpson, Eleanor Walk**

OPERATIONS

Operations Director **Jo Topping**
Visitor Experience Manager **Lynne Yates**
Deputy Visitor Experience Manager **Stuart Galligan**
Assistant Visitor Experience Manager **Rachel Davies**
Head of Facilities **David Mitchell**
Maintenance Technician **Carl Johnson**
IT Manager **Ean Burgon**
IT Support & Network Technician **John Barlow**
Volunteer Coordinator **Kate Hardy**
Hires and Events Assistant **Amelia Bayliss**
Deputy Retail Manager **Gail Owen**
Shop Assistants **Elisa Robinson, Clare Sidebotham, Amber Samuels, Emily Tilzey, Jessica Sharp**

Duty Managers **Jill Bridgeman, Helen Coyne, Rachel Davies**
Head Ushers **Tracey Fleet, Heather Madden, Stuart Shaw**
Security **Liam Ainsworth, Liam Carty, Dave Hughes, Mike Seal**
Stage Door **Thomas Flaherty**
Ushers **Tom Banks, Georgie Brown, Helen Brown, Natasha Bybik, Elizabeth Callan, Liam Carty, Emily Chadwick, Richard Challinor, Alicia Cole, Elizabeth Coupe, Chris Dance, Anna Davenport, Cliona Donohue, Luther Edmead, Harry Egan, Amy Claire Evans, Paul Evans, Neil Fenton, Beth Galligan, Wesley Harding, Connie Hartley, Jennifer Hulman, Dan Lizar, Ben Lucas, Heather Madden, Sue McGonnell, Tony O'Driscoll, Elle Pemberton Steer, Alice Proctor, John Roy, Stuart Shaw, Vincent Tuohy, Edward (Ted) Walker, Judith Wood, Mahdi Zadeh**
Cleaning Contractors:
Head Cleaner **Lillian Williams**
Cleaners **Gillian Bradshaw, Susan Burroughs, Elaine Connolly, Valarie Daffern, Jackie Farnell, Ahab Mohamed, Maryam Murmin, Daniel Thompson, Hussein Fatima Yassin**

PRODUCTION

Head of Production **Simon Curtis**
Props Buyer **Kim Ford**
Production Coordinator **Greg Skipworth**
Driver **John Fisher**
Head of Technical **Richard Delight**
Head of Sound **Sorcha Williams**
Senior Sound Technicians **Sam Leahy, Matt Sims**
Sound Technicians **Catrin Petersson**
Head of Lighting **Mark Distin-Webster**
Senior Lighting Technicians **Matthew Lever**
Lighting Technicians **Louise Anderson, Connor Skelton**
Stage Technicians **Simon Wild, Luke Murray, Edward Hingley**
Head of Props and Settings **Neil Gidley**
Deputy Head of Props and Settings **Andy Bubble**
Workshop Supervisor **Carl Heston**
Senior Scenic Artist **Phil Costello**
Prop Makers **Ben Cook, Stuart Mitchell, Sarah Worrall**
Hires & Events Assistant **Amelia Bayliss**

Head of Wardrobe **Nikki Meredith**
Deputy Head of Wardrobe **Tracy Dunk**
Studio Wardrobe Supervisor **Felicia Jagne**
Tailor & Gents Cutter **Rose Calderbank**
Cutters **Jennifer Adgey, Rachel Bailey**
Hair and Makeup Supervisor **Jo Shepstone**
Costume Hire Manager **Ludmila Krzak**
With help from the volunteer team

PROGRAMME

Senior Producer **Ric Watts**
Head of Casting & Associate Director **Jerry Knight-Smith CDG**
Company Manager **Lee Gower-Drinkwater**
Dramaturg **Suzanne Bell**
Producer **Amy Clewes**
Artist Development Administrator **Grace Ng-Ralph**
Bruntwood Prize Coordinator **Chloe Smith**
Assistant Producer **Max Emmerson**
Associate Casting Director **Vicky Richardson**

THE RIVALS BAR & RESTAURANT

Adam Abreu, Mark Beattie, Victoria Bowen, Leah Curran, Nick Edmead, Anna Fysh, Jose Garcia, Emma Gold, Rupert Hill, Sarah Hope, Tom Johnson, James Langrish, Malgorzata Langrish, Joseph Lester, Robin Lyons, Simon Mayne, Elle Pemberton, Helen Thomason, Damian Traczyk, Jake Tysome, Christopher Wilson

VOLUNTEEERS

Sally Almond, Diane Amans, Anne Barnaby, Joan Beverly, Christine Brown, Nim Burgen, Noreen Burns, Pamela Burrow, Jim Capewell, Eileen Carleton, Claire Chatterton, Geoffrey Clifton, Norma Code, Joan Cowlishaw, Pat Cross, Salle Dare, Pat Dexter, Terry Donnelly, Beverley Dowling, Gill Edmondson, Maggie Evans, Claire Fern, Mary Findlay, Mildred Finney, Doreen Firth, Anne Fitzpatrick, Barbara Frankl, McGirr Georgia, Irene Gibbons, Norman Goodman, Irene Gray, Sue Hall Smith, Kate Sharples, Sylvia Hampton, Carolyn Harrison, Margaret Hatton, Enid Head, Margaret Higson, Grace Jackson, Julia Jessup, Jean Johnson, Pat Jones, Liz Kenny, Judith Khoudi, Debrah Lamb, Ann Laza, Jean Lea, Sheila Lorca, Stella Lowe, Sheila Lowe, Lillian Mills, Helen Mitchell, Hilary Murray, John Pearsall, Robert Pegrum, Adrian

DIRECTOR'S NOTE

I was sent an early draft of Kendall Feaver's *The Almighty Sometimes* in 2016 and immediately knew I wanted to direct it, not just because it tackles one of the most pressing social issues of our time - children's mental health – but also because of Kendall's strong voice as she explores the fragile relationship of a mother and her teenage daughter on the cusp of adulthood. Renee and Anna are strong women with a biting wit; as they negotiate and re-evaluate their relationship, their love and at times loathing for each other is real and visceral. Their dilemmas are universal: Renee questioning if she has done her best for her child and whether the choices she made were in her best interests; and Anna trying to take control of her own life and figure out who she really is.

The fact that Anna is receiving medical treatment for a mental health problem that manifested itself in early childhood adds a potent dimension to their relationship and to the play. The more I have delved into the world of the play and researched mental health, the more I have come to understand how large and complex a problem this is here in the UK, especially against a background of cuts to CAMHS, the adolescent health care service. This support is becoming increasingly hard to come by and I feel this is exactly the right time to be doing this play.

In working on the play, we met many young people growing up with mental health issues, and the families and professionals who dedicate their lives to caring and supporting them. It was important to me to hear their voices and understand their experiences. It is clear that everyone is different and there is no single treatment suitable for all; many people's lives are improved by medication, while others find help in other ways such as talking therapies. For many young people on medication, the dilemma of 'What is me and what is the medication?' seems to be a recurring question. This play tells the story of a unique experience and does not seek to give answers; it is not representative of everyone's story, but I hope that it will shine a light on families coping with mental illness, and that it will encourage a conversation about how we as a society look after our young people with mental health problems.

Katy Rudd, Director

The Almighty Sometimes

Kendall Feaver won the Judges Award at the 2015 Bruntwood Prize for Playwriting for her play *The Almighty Sometimes*. After the Royal Exchange, a second production will follow at Griffin Theatre Company, Sydney. Kendall graduated with a Master's in Writing for Performance from Goldsmiths, University of London, supported by an Ian Potter Cultural Trust Award. She has been on attachment at the National Theatre Studio and is developing an original musical as part of the National Theatre's Musical Theatre Group. *The Almighty Sometimes* is Kendall's first professional production.

KENDALL FEAVER

The Almighty Sometimes

FABER & FABER

First published in 2018
by Faber and Faber Ltd
74–77 Great Russell Street
London WC1B 3DA

Typeset by Country Setting, Kingsdown, Kent CT14 8ES
Printed in England by CPI Group (UK) Ltd, Croydon CR0 4YY

A CIP record for this book is available from the British Library

978-0-571-34724-7

2 4 6 8 10 9 7 5 3 1

Jennifer Hordern
*mother, friend, and autonomous individual,
this play is for you*

Acknowledgements

Katy Rudd; Suzanne Bell; Sarah Frankcom and the entire
team at the Royal Exchange Theatre; Kirsten Foster at
Casarotto Ramsay; William Lewis; Sharon Duncan-
Brewster, Julie Hesmondhalgh, Norah Lopez Holden and
Mike Noble; the judges, readers and fellow winners (now
friends) of the 2015 Bruntwood Award; Nick Sidi and
Elliott Harper Productions; Lee Lewis and Ben Winspear
at Griffin Theatre Company; my Australian Family:
Kevin, Jennie and Sam Feaver; my English family: Kevin,
Nicola, and Jane Lewis; Liz Arday, Corinne Furlong,
Luke Rogers and Tiffany Woodsmith; Madeleine Postle;
John Ginman, David Lane and classmates at Goldsmiths,
University of London; The Australia Council for the Arts,
the Ian Potter Cultural Trust and John and Yvonne
Almgren; Katie Randall, Harrison Haggith and Ailsa
Brown for pushing me to finish this; James Young for the
swear-words; the many psychiatrists, psychologists,
parents and service users for their time, insights and
expert advice, particularly Professor Jonathan Green,
Dr Sara Davies and Ginny Allende-Cullen; and the many
many brilliant actors who workshopped or read this
script over the past five years, especially Niamh Cusack,
Patsy Ferran and Josie Walker.

Lastly, I'd like to acknowledge the work of the following
authors: James Davies, Terri Cheney, Dr David Healy,
Marya Hornbacher, Dr Joanna Moncrieff, Dr Demitri
and Janice Papolos, Judith Warner and Robert Whittaker.

The **Almighty Sometimes** was first presented at the Royal Exchange Theatre, Manchester, on 9 February 2018. The cast, in alphabetical order, was as follows:

Vivienne Sharon Duncan-Brewster
Renee Julie Hesmondhalgh
Anna Norah Lopez Holden
Oliver Mike Noble

Director Katy Rudd
Designer Rosanna Vize
Lighting Lucy Carter
Sound Giles Thomas
Movement Vicki Manderson
Casting Directors Jerry Knight-Smith CDG
   and Vicky Richardson
Assistant Director Atri Bannerjee

Characters

Renee
late forties to mid-fifties

Anna
eighteen

Oliver
twenty-one

Vivienne
mid- to late forties

Notes

The action is set in various locations.
These do not have to be more than suggested.

Each scene begins and ends abruptly
as indicated by the horizontal rules.

THE ALMIGHTY SOMETIMES

Maybe sometimes your child will say that they will kill themselves. This is something to take seriously . . . If your child gets these thoughts, ask the doctor for Zyprexa, or something like that. If this situation ever happens, hold them still until they calm down and stop wanting to kill themselves.

Hold them until they feel a part of this world.

Advice from a nine-year-old girl, quoted in Demitri F. Papolos, and Janice Papolos, *The Bipolar Child: The Definitive and Reassuring Guide to Childhood's Most Misunderstood Disorder* (2002)

This text went to press before the end of rehearsals and so may differ slightly from the play as performed.

Act One

Vivienne (*reading*) 'When the girl was old enough to walk, she began to float, two or three inches above the ground, and then higher and higher until her head hit the ceiling and her mother had to buy an extra-extendable ladder just to bring her down. "You must keep it a secret," the neighbours said, so the mother tied a piece of string from the girl's hand to her own, and let down the bottom of every skirt, so no one could see the space between the shoes and the floor.

'One day, the mother forgot to lock the kitchen drawer, and the girl found a knife, a big knife, the best knife, for old bread and tough legs of ham, and she dragged it down her body, top to bottom, opening herself like a leather bag. She stepped out of her skin and kicked it away, where it hit the wall – splat! – and slithered to the ground. The mother tried to catch her daughter but there was nothing there to hold on to.

' "Look up, look up, look up," the little girl said, and she flew around her mother, and did somersaults in the air, and walked along the clothes-line, and made silly faces at the window, while the mother cried, and the skin turned to slush in her hands.'

Anna Do you want something to eat?

Oliver No, I'm good, thanks.

Anna You sure? I can totally get you something to eat.

Oliver Nah, I'm OK.

Anna You must be starving – only thing Izzy put out was a bowl of crisps.

Oliver Had dinner before I left, so.

Anna That was like five hours ago.

Oliver And that's a long time, is it?

Anna I mean . . . not for everyone.

Oliver No?

Anna Not if you're like – I don't know – a camel-herder.

Oliver A camel-herder?

Anna You know: wandering across the Sahara Desert. I bet those guys hardly ever stop to eat.

Oliver Sure, I mean, I guess that's / true . . .

Anna Or maybe you're a member of a strict religious community where, like, a fundamental rule of your ancient belief system is that you periodically starve yourself. Or *maybe* you've been arrested for drug smuggling in some obscure South-East Asian country so you're sitting in this overcrowded prison that hasn't subscribed to any declaration of basic human rights, but for everyone else . . . yeah . . . five hours is a long time.

She hands him a bowl of stew.

Oliver What is it?

Anna My mum made it. It's got aubergine in it. Tomatoes and vinegar too. It's been in the fridge for three days now, and I know that sounds horrible, like borderline offensive, but something kind of magical happens to it, and I'm not sure if it's meant to – like it's a dish that requires some Jesus-like resurrection before it gets going – or maybe Mum's got so much vinegar in there it's basically embalming itself – whatever the reason, it *genuinely* gets better the longer it's sat there. (*Beat.*) Do you want some?

Oliver No, I'm uh, I'm still OK . . . thanks.

Anna shrugs and continues eating it herself. Oliver takes a few moments to look around the room.

So . . .

Anna So . . .

Oliver You live with your mum then?

Anna What makes you say that?

Oliver She's still cooking for you, so . . .

Anna She likes to cook.

Oliver Just lets herself in and –

Anna Sure.

Oliver OK . . . What about the house?

Anna What about it?

Oliver It's nice.

Anna Nice?

Oliver Classy.

Anna And . . . what? You don't think I'm –

Oliver No, no, I do –

Anna Because I can be classy –

Oliver In like twenty years, yeah. In twenty years you'll be so classy.

Anna And now?

Oliver Now? I dunno. Now you're not supposed to have things like that – whatever that thing is.

Anna It's a diffuser. *(Beat.)* Makes the room smell nice.

Oliver That's what deodorant's for.

Anna Deodorant's for under your arms.

Oliver Sure, but when you're finished there, you spray a bit of it round the room – freshens it right up, doesn't it? (*Wanders a bit, stops.*) Also: you have a bunch of photos on the wall of you as a baby, so if it's just you living here, that's a bit fucking weird.

 Anna grins.

Is your mum here now?

Anna Asleep, yeah.

Oliver How far away is she?

Anna Like, in feet, or –

Oliver No, just . . . roughly.

Anna She's upstairs.

Oliver And where's your bedroom?

Anna Down the hall there.

Oliver So kind of underneath it?

Anna Yeah.

Oliver Not sure how I feel about that.

Anna About what?

Oliver Your mum . . . above us.

Anna I don't understand.

Oliver Sleeping above us, while we're, you know –

Anna What?

Oliver You know . . .

 Beat.

Anna Excuse me?!

Oliver Wait . . . what?

Anna You think we're having sex tonight?

Oliver Um. Kind of assumed, yeah.

Anna Why would you do that?

Oliver I just walked you home.

Anna So?

Oliver Kind of a long way . . .

Anna And that entitles you to –

Oliver It doesn't *entitle* me to –

Anna Because you seem to be implying –

Oliver I'm not implying!

Anna – that I should give you something in return.

   Silence.

Oliver Look: I'm sorry, OK? You're right. I shouldn't have *assumed*. I thought . . . *maybe*? But I shouldn't have *assumed*, that that was, what was, going to . . .

   Anna smiles.

I hate you.

Anna No you don't.

Oliver No, I do. I hate you.

Anna You don't even remember me.

Oliver Were you this mean at school?

Anna Is that what you think of me?

Oliver Nah, not really. (*Beat.*) I was joking.

Anna Joking.

Oliver Yeah, like you were with the whole 'not having sex' thing. A joke, right?

Anna What do you think of me?

Oliver Huh?

Anna What do you think of me?

Oliver Like you said: don't really remember you, so . . .

Anna So your current opinion of me is completely uninfluenced by experience.

Oliver Uh . . . I guess so.

Anna Based on nothing but observation.

Oliver Sure.

Anna What do you think of me?

   Pause.

Oliver I think you're very attractive.

Anna Nothing physical.

Oliver OK.

Anna Nothing relating to the body.

Oliver I know what physical means.

Anna You can say whatever you want.

Oliver Kind of feeling the pressure though.

Anna I won't be offended.

Oliver And what if you are?

Anna I promise I'll have sex with you anyway.

   Beat.

Oliver OK. You talk a lot.

Anna No, I don't.

Oliver Kind of hard to get a word in edgeways –

Anna That's bullshit – (*Beat.*) OK.

Oliver You're confident. Funny. I mean, some people might not find you funny –

Anna Like who?

Oliver The people you bulldoze with all that talking.

Anna Right.

Oliver But you're also, I dunno . . .

Anna What?

Oliver Brave.

Anna Brave?

Oliver I think so, yeah.

Anna I don't think I'm brave.

Oliver Well not like *Braveheart* brave. Not like 'wearing a kilt in the middle of fucking winter' brave. Just kind of, I dunno . . . determined?

Anna Determined?

Oliver Yeah, like earlier, we were in the pantry stealing that wine, and Izzy was just outside and she said: 'What the fuck is Anna doing here?' (*Beat.*) No? Thought you would have heard that.

Anna I did. Was hoping you hadn't.

Oliver Well . . . that's brave, see? Most people would have gone home at that point.

Anna Do you think I – (*Beat.*) Should I / have?

Oliver What? God – no. Seriously. If you'd left then, I never would have walked you home – and not because

I didn't want to – just because we'd only known each other for like . . . five minutes – and I need at least four or five hours – and I'm talking four or five hours *minimum* – before I can pluck up the courage to . . . you know –

He moves towards her, kisses her.

– taste your mum's cooking.

He licks or dabs at the side of his mouth.

Anna It's good, isn't it?

Oliver Yeah, it's um . . . it's pretty great, yeah.

He kisses her again. And again. And again and again. The lights come on.

Renee Oh my God –

Anna Mum!

Renee I'm so sorry –

Anna Mum, get out!

Renee Sorry, I'll just –

Anna Mum!

Renee Anna – give me a sec, OK?! (*Stops.*) Oliver?

Oliver Hi.

Renee How are you?

Oliver Fine, thank you.

Renee I haven't seen you since you were –

Oliver A kid, yeah.

Renee You've grown.

Oliver Thank you. I mean, yes, I have.

Beat, several moments too long.

Anna (*to Renee*) What? Why are you still standing there?

Oliver I should go.

Anna No!

Oliver No, no, I should go.

Anna You don't have to do that.

Oliver I think I should, yeah.

Anna No. Really. Mum will go back to her room; we'll go to mine. OK?

Oliver I mean . . . sure, yeah, if it's OK with your mum –

    Beat.

Renee She does have work in the morning, so –

Anna Mum!

Renee I'm just reminding you in case you've forgotten.

Anna Great, thank you.

Renee Your rota is on the fridge, it says you have work in the morning.

Anna That's none of your business!

Renee Kate is my friend.

Anna She's also my boss.

Renee I got you the job.

Anna Would you get out of here?!

    She stares at Renee, willing her to leave.

Renee OK, OK, I'm going, I'm going. (*Moves towards the door.*) It was nice seeing you again, Oliver.

Oliver Yeah, you too. And I'm sorry, you know, if we woke you up –

Renee It's fine, don't worry about it.

Oliver We've both uh, we've both had a bit to drink so –

Renee / Excuse me?

Anna (*to Renee*) I haven't.

Beat.

Oliver Sorry, I don't, um –

Anna I haven't had anything to drink.

Oliver We took that / wine from –

Anna Doesn't mean I had any of it.

Silence.
Oliver looks between Anna and Renee, hopelessly confused.

Oliver Sorry, I'm uh . . . just to be honest with you: I – me – *just* me – have – had – a bit to drink. Like, not so much I'm going to pass out or anything, but maybe, um, maybe a bit too much to completely understand this conversation, so . . .

He motions towards the direction of the door.

It was um, nice to see you again, Mrs –

Renee Renee.

Oliver Sure. Yeah. OK.

Renee You can call me Renee.

Oliver I mean, yeah, OK, if you want.

Renee It's my name, Oliver.

Oliver Sure, realise that, yeah. Just a bit weird, isn't it?

Calling you that: *Renee*. Like you're an actual, you know –

Renee Person?

Anna Mum.

Beat.

Renee I'm sorry – Oliver, you don't have to leave.

Oliver No, it's OK –

Renee You can stay on the sofa if you want to?

Oliver No, I don't live that far away, so –

Renee Let me call you a taxi at least –

Oliver No, no, it's OK, I'll go, I'm going. Sorry to wake you, Mrs – Renee – sorry to –

Anna I'll walk you out.

Oliver Sure, that'd be great, yeah.

Anna exits with Oliver, leaving Renee alone in the living room.
    Renee tightens her dressing gown and smiles a bit. After a few moments, Anna re-enters.

Anna I wasn't drinking.

Renee I know.

Anna Sometimes I pour myself a glass so they don't ask questions, but I don't ever –

Renee It's OK. I believe you.

Pause.

So.
    You're having sex now.

Anna Oh God –

Renee I know, I know. I did suspect it was happening, I mean, it was one of those things I assumed *had* happened, but I wasn't sure where, or when, or with whom, and that's kind of how I hoped things would stay: you know, somewhat *vague* on the details –

Anna I'm actually really happy to keep it that way?

Renee Wonderful. So am I.

She grins at Anna. Anna struggles not to.

How was the party anyway?

Anna It was fine.

Renee What about Isabel? How's she finding Edinburgh?

Anna I don't know.

Renee You didn't ask her?

Anna I didn't really talk to her.

Renee She's been away for three months –

Anna And it's not like anything exciting has happened –

Renee She moved cities, started university –

Anna I meant to me.

Beat.

Renee Anna –

Anna No – Mum –

Renee – this is what happens after school –

Anna (*settling in*) Ohhkay.

Renee You make different choices. Some of us go to university, some us don't, and if you don't, it's nothing to be embarrassed about –

Anna I'm not embarrassed.

Renee OK.

Anna I'm not embarrassed, Mum.

Renee I'm really glad to hear that.

Anna I'm actually thinking about applying this year, so . . .

   Beat.

Renee Applying where? Edinburgh?

Anna No. (*Pause; carefully.*) Leeds, maybe. Or Hull. I've also been thinking about Swansea?

Renee Swansea??

Anna Yeah.

Renee We don't know anyone in *Swansea*.

Anna Which is kind of what's so great about it.

Renee Have you been thinking about this for a while, or –

Anna A couple of months.

Renee How long would the drive take?

Anna I'm not really sure –

Renee The train is at least four hours –

Anna I guess . . .

Renee Which is kind of a long way, don't you think?

Anna I mean, no, not really: Erin is at Nottingham – April is at Plymouth – that's even further away – and Hannah McCulloch is going to Italy next year on an exchange programme, and if she can go halfway across Europe –

Renee But what does Hannah McCulloch have to do with you?

29

Anna I'm just saying: if Hannah McCulloch can go all the way to Italy –

Renee Yes, but Hannah McCulloch – as far as I'm aware – has never been diagnosed –

Anna *Mum.*

Silence. Anna is visibly wounded.

Renee I'm sorry, love, but . . . be reasonable, OK? I have to remind you to take your medication as it is, you barely keep to your sleep schedule – what is it now? (*Checks her watch.*) Almost 2.30 in the morning – and you think you're ready to move four hours away? By yourself?

—

Look: I'm not saying no –

Anna No, no, I think that's exactly what you're saying –

Renee Anna, if you're going to get yourself all worked up –

Anna I'm not worked up –

Renee You certainly look like you're heading there –

Anna Mum, I'm – (*She takes a breath, steadies herself.*) I'm fine – (*Raises her hands in surrender.*) Look – I'm fine.

She lowers her arms. Silence.

You know it is kind of disturbing that you don't want me to do anything with my life –

Renee Do you really think that's what I want, Anna?

—

If you went to university, love . . . I would be *thrilled.* I just think we can find you something a little closer to home.

———————

Anna It's good, isn't it? I knew I liked to write, I didn't know I was any good at it.

Vivienne You were a very bright little girl.

Anna Not bright.

Vivienne No?

Anna I was *brilliant*: the knife, the skin, how she does away with it – those are some pretty abstract connections.

Vivienne They are.

Anna Which is advanced for an eight-year-old.

Vivienne (*amused*) You've decided that, have you?

Anna I mean: I'm no expert on this stuff – I haven't studied it like you have – but I'm *guessing* that's advanced, right?

Vivienne Well . . . most eight-year-olds do tend focus on the obvious: Bob is a man, Bob has a hat, the hat is brown, Bob likes his hat –

Anna But when *I* was eight years old –

Vivienne Anna . . .

  Beat.

Anna Sorry. Did you have anything else you wanted to say?

Vivienne No, but when you ask a question, you need to listen to the answer.

Anna Sorry. Understood. Can I . . . ?

Vivienne Go ahead.

Anna (*launching in*) But when *I* was eight years old, I could fill a whole notebook with stories. And this isn't the only one. I was going through Mum's wardrobe looking for a pair of her shoes –

Vivienne Which are lovely by the way –

Anna Thank you! I was looking for these and I found something much better. Hundreds of notebooks, loose sheets of paper – all categorised in shoeboxes by the age I was when I wrote them. Mum's kept them all, and I was surprised at that, because Mum hates looking backwards – she'll buy a whole new bottle of milk before she'll let the old one reach its use-by date – but for some reason, she kept these – I've spent most of the night reading them – and they're just – I mean, the ones around four are mostly illegible – but seven, eight, nine, ten are just . . .

Anna scans the page again.

(*Reading.*) ' "Look up, look up, look up," the little girl said, and she flew around her mother, and did somersaults in the air, and walked along the clothes-line, and made silly faces at the window, while the mother cried, and the skin turned to slush in her hands.'
I was eight! *Eight!*

Vivienne Like I said, you were a very bright little girl.

Anna (*scrambling through the pages*) Do you want me to read you another one?

Vivienne We don't really have time, I'm sorry –

Anna (*scrambling though the pages*) Just one more –

Vivienne No / Anna –

Anna 'Bang! Into the water they dived –'

Vivienne (*with emphasis*) Anna, I need to talk you.

Beat.

Anna Is something wrong?

Vivienne Nothing's wrong –

Anna Because when people say 'I need to talk to you' –

Vivienne Anna, sit down –

Anna Because I might fall over in shock?

Vivienne Because we need to have a conversation.

She taps the chair across from her and Anna sits down.

Anna . . . (*Pause. Carefully.*) Someone with my training wouldn't normally see a patient past the age of eighteen.

Anna (*processing this*) OK . . . but I've, um . . . I've been eighteen for a while –

Vivienne Yes, I know. And you have been stable for so long –

Anna I have, yeah.

Vivienne You've proven to me that you can deal with change and cope with stress –

Anna No, no, I can – I can definitely do that –

Vivienne – which is why I know you'll manage the transition to a new psychiatrist –

Anna A new –

Vivienne An *adult* psychiatrist.

Beat.

Anna, I don't want you to worry about this, OK? The timing can vary from patient to patient. I can transition you to Adult Services now if you like, but we can also work towards this over the next six to eight months, whichever you prefer.

Anna Sorry, I thought you . . . (*Beat.*) I thought you were going to tell me I didn't need the pills any more.

—

I've been on them for seven years; surely it's worked by now.

Vivienne You have an illness, Anna.

Anna But I'm older now. I'm stronger. How do you know I haven't sorted out some natural equilibrium all on my own? Maybe we should try it, just for a bit –

Vivienne I don't think so –

Anna We'll do it for science! Test a hypothesis!

Vivienne Anna –

Anna You can't stop me, you know. If I wanted to, I could just stop taking them.

   Beat.

Vivienne Listen to me, and listen very carefully. That medication has been in your body for seven years. And your body has adapted to that, learnt to process it, and most importantly, has learnt to expect it. If you stop taking them, Anna, you won't just regress, you'll plummet.

Anna So when I'm thirty, when I'm forty, when I'm celebrating my first and only centenary, I'll still be popping pills?

Vivienne Not necessarily – if you've been stable for a long period of time –

Anna And I have – you said so yourself –

Vivienne – then the medication can be tapered off, but this is not the right moment, Anna. You're about to move to a new doctor –

Anna I don't want a new doctor!

   Pause.

Vivienne I'm supposed to recommend someone else.

Anna Says who?

Vivienne It's just how the system works.

Anna Because I hit eighteen and – what? – I become this completely different person?

Vivienne No, but –

Anna So can't you make an exception?

Vivienne On the basis of what?

Anna I don't know: that leaving my doctor of seven years would be a bit fucking shit –

Vivienne Yes! Yes, it is a bit fucking shit. And completely arbitrary – more to do with funding than anything you – the patient – may or may not *actually* need, but – (*Beat.*) I'm sorry, Anna. I can't justify it any longer.

> *Pause.*

I'm not going to send you to just anyone. I will find someone – someone I trust – and I will make sure you are taken care of, OK?
> Anna?

Anna OK.

> *Silence.*

Vivienne You look tired.

Anna I'm not.

Vivienne Have you been sleeping well?

Anna Yes.

Vivienne Are you sure?

Anna Right through the night, I promise.

Vivienne And the nightmares?

> *Beat.*

Anna?

Anna Just little things now.

Vivienne Like what?

Anna My hand is burning and I can't take it off the stove. I add milk to my tea but it clumps together and floats in my cup. I'm driving and I see Dad walking down the side of the road, but I don't have time to stop so I –

Vivienne You've had that one before.

Anna But it's not as bad now. There's no gore, no bits. He doesn't break: he scatters.

Vivienne Scatters?

Anna Little particles. Everywhere. He's not blood or bone. He's dust. I don't get out of the car because I'm scared I'll breathe him in.

Silence.

Vivienne Let's take you up again –

Anna No!

Vivienne Just 25 mills.

Anna Anything over 6 makes my hands shake.

Vivienne That was the Risperidone. You haven't had any side-effects on the Quetiapine.

Anna If I go up another 25 milligrams, I bet I'll discover one.

Vivienne Let me add it to your prescription at least.

Anna I won't take it.

Vivienne Whether you do or not is entirely up to you. But if your nightmares get worse, I won't have you waiting another six weeks before you can do something about it.

She writes the prescription while Anna collects her things.

By the way . . . your mum phoned.

Anna stops.

Swansea?

Anna It doesn't have to be Swansea . . .

Vivienne She's worried you're not ready.

Anna Yeah? And what did you say to that?

Vivienne I said: as your daughter is eighteen years old now, it's no longer appropriate for me to discuss this with anyone but Anna.

Anna (*beat*) You didn't . . .

Vivienne I did.

Anna *And?*

Vivienne And?

Anna What do you think?

Vivienne Well . . . If it's university you're interested in – not Swansea itself – I suppose I'm not entirely sure what the problem is. I can't think of a single writer, living or dead, who felt they had to move two hundred miles away just to pick up a pen . . .

Anna You think I can be a writer, Vivi?

Vivienne (*handing over the prescription*) At the risk of fuelling that already high opinion of yourself . . . you really were an exceptional little girl.

———————————

Anna (*reading*) 'Bang! Into the water they dived – and the parents cheered from the side of the pool – even though they knew that their children would sink and

37

drown and would never beat Arabelle – because although
Arabelle suffered from a rare and incurable disease that
prevented her from walking – in the water, she was
supersonic. She could swim two laps of the pool without
ever needing to take a breath – a skill she practised every
night in the bathtub – one minute, two minutes, three
minutes, four – and as she lay underneath the surface
trying for a record five – she began to imagine she was
something else entirely – a blue-ringed octopus, maybe,
or a giant squid, or a hammerhead shark, or an electric
eel – but if she absolutely had to choose, she would
become a deep-sea-humpback-anglerfish with the
crooked teeth and the droopy light on the top of its head,
because she quite liked the cold, and she didn't mind the
dark, and if you had a lamp on the top of your head then
you'd always have a light to read by, and this was
definitely something she'd need to consider if she ever
decided to –'

Renee Afternoon.

—

Productive day, I hope?

—

The writing, is it going well?

Anna Yes.

Renee Are you nearly finished?

Anna I only started a week ago.

Renee So how much longer?

Anna As long as it takes.

Renee And how long do these things usually take?

Anna It took Jack Kerouac three weeks to write *On the
Road*.

Renee OK . . .

Anna It took Jane Austen sixteen years to write *Pride and Prejudice*.

Renee And who are you: Jack or Jane?

Anna I don't know yet.

Renee Well, when you find out . . .

Anna What do you care?

Renee Just wondering when I'll get my kitchen back.

Anna I can't write in my room. It's too messy in there.

    Renee eyeballs the mess on the floor. She moves to sit.

Anna No no no –

Renee What?

Anna Don't sit!

Renee I need to talk to you.

Anna I'll lose my train of thought.

Renee So finish it, and then we'll talk.

    Beat.

Anna Well, it's gone now, hasn't it?!

Renee Can't have been that important then.

    She makes herself comfortable.

I bumped into Kate at school. Strange to see her there.

Anna I'm sure she picks up her kids at least once a week.

Renee I mean I didn't *expect* to see her. I didn't *organise* to see her. It just happened.

    —

She asked after you.

—

I told her you were well.

—

She said that you could have your job back if you wanted it.

Anna Just came out and said that, did she?

Renee Yes.

Anna Walked across the playground and said: 'Hey there! Tell Anna she can have her job back.'

Renee More or less.

Anna Well, if you just *happen* to bump into her again, you can tell her I don't want it.

Renee Not even part-time?

Anna No.

Renee But what about money?

Anna What about it?

Renee How are you going to support yourself?

Anna Well . . . you did offer to pay for me to stay in halls if I picked a university that was close by . . .

Renee Ah! So by *that* logic I can pay for you to stay in my living room.

Anna ignores her, carries on working.

Anna, I'd, uh . . . I'd be interested to know what Vivienne thinks about all this –

Anna She thinks it's great.

Renee (*unconvinced*) Really?

Anna She thinks I'm an exceptional writer, actually.

Renee Maybe I should call her –

Anna She won't talk to you.

—

It's not personal.

Renee I know.

Anna It's just the way things are now.

Silence.

Renee I found Oliver in the hallway last night.

—

Is he over much?

Anna Most nights.

Renee Going well?

Anna I guess so.

Renee He knows he can come over before midnight, right?

Anna He's probably scared he'll see you.

Renee (*beat*) Right. Yes. I imagine he is.

—

I'm sorry, Anna.

Anna For what?

Renee For after the party . . . for embarrassing you like that . . . in front of Oliver. I should have waited until the morning –

Anna To embarrass me?

Renee To say hello. And I would have been incredibly *cool* about it too – no jokes, no innuendo. Hopefully you'll give me another chance to prove myself . . .?

—

(*Indicating the notebook.*) Can I read some of it?

Anna No.

Renee I'd really like to read some of it.

Anna It's not ready.

Renee (*picking up some of the papers*) Just a bit of it –

Anna (*taking them back*) Mum! I said –

Her phone rings; she answers.

Hey! Yeah – no, no – just give me a second to, um –

Anna glances back to Renee who waves her off. Anna exits with the phone.
Renee sits in silence. After a few moments she moves over to the notebook and opens it. She flicks through the pages, which are almost entirely blank.
Anna re-enters and watches her.

Anna It's hard.

Renee (*putting the notebook down*) What is?

Anna Writing.

Renee I imagine it is, yes.

Anna But it's harder for me, I think.

Renee How so?

Anna I'm having trouble with thoughts, normal thoughts. They get kind of . . . stuck . . . half out. And some words, some really simple words, I know them – I know I know them! – but I can't bring them, you know . . . up.

Renee And what does Vivienne have to say about it?

Anna I haven't told her.

Renee Why not?

Anna She'll try and get me to take something for it.

Renee I mean . . . (*Beat.*) If she thinks it would help –

Anna I'm fine, Mum.

Renee I didn't say you weren't –

Anna I'm fine!

Renee OK, OK –

Anna I just can't write anything!

Renee Well, maybe you never could!

    Beat.

Anna Excuse me?

Renee I'm just saying: you've changed your entire life to satisfy what – some childhood habit? – and perhaps that's all it was, all it ever was, and there's no shame in admitting that.

    Anna opens up her backpack and pulls out some old notebooks.

Anna Look. Look at this.

Renee Where did you get these?

Anna Read it, Mum.

Renee Have you been going through my things?

Anna (*reading*) 'Arabelle sank and the colours changed from blue to green to black –'

Renee Anna –

Anna (*reading*) '– and then she was 4,000 metres under the surface – the top of the Abyssopelagic Zone –'

Renee Anna, please –

Anna '– where the pressure can bend your bones, and crush your lungs, and make your head crumple like a paper –'

Renee ANNA.

Anna What?

Renee I've read these. I don't need to hear them again –

Anna They're *amazing* –

Renee They're terrifying.

Beat.

Anna But you kept them – whole boxes of them –

Renee For assessments.

Anna What do you mean, 'assessments'?

Renee You were so young; it was difficult getting anyone to see you.

Beat. Anna realises.

Anna You used them to prove I was ill.

—

Do you not understand how advanced these are?

Renee They were written by a very sick little girl.

Anna They were written by me!

Renee At a time when the illness was starting to take hold.

Anna The illness? Are you serious? The illness?!

Renee Yes. The illness.

Anna The illness cannot write, Mother. The illness does not have an imagination. The illness cannot think of an idea, then sit down and pick up a pencil, because illnesses, unlike people, do not have opposable thumbs!

44

Renee You were seven years old the first time you attempted.

Anna Oh God, Mum!

Renee Seven.

Anna It wasn't that serious!

Renee You wrote a six-page manifesto bequeathing toys to your friends and then you jumped out the bedroom window.

Anna My bedroom was on the ground floor.

Renee Luckily!

Anna I fell three feet.

Renee You broke your arm.

Anna Most kids do at some point.

Renee Not of their own volition!

Anna You over-reacted. Everyone over-reacted.

Renee I raced outside to find you, and you weren't screaming, you weren't crying, you just seemed so disappointed: 'Mummy,' you said. 'I didn't think you'd be in heaven!'

Beat. Anna sniggers.

It's not funny.

Anna It is a bit.

Renee It's not.

Anna Alright, it's not!

Renee Put them away, Anna.

Anna No.

Renee Then I'll take them, I should have thrown them out years ago –

Anna gathers them all up and holds them to her chest. Silence.

Did something happen at that party, Anna?

—

Did someone say something to you that made you feel in any way less successful?

—

If they did, I want you to know how proud I am of you and everything you have achieved – because even the smallest of your achievements are made significantly more impressive knowing the debilitating disorder you have worked against. And you have *worked*, Anna, you have worked so hard, to reach this point – this wonderful tenuous place – where now – now you can't even notice it. You have never been stronger, smarter or more capable than you are now, and if that isn't worth two-and-a-half of Hannah McCulloch and her passable-at-best Italian, I don't know what is.

Anna Do you mean that?

Renee Of course I do.

Anna This is the best I've ever been?

Renee Absolutely.

Anna You can't notice it any more?

Renee No, Anna. Not at all.

Anna Good. Because I haven't taken pills for almost a week and I was worried you might have twigged.

Silence.

Renee takes out her mobile phone and begins looking for a number.

Anna Mum, what are you –

_____

Vivienne You lied to me.

Anna I didn't *lie* to you –

Vivienne We talked about this, Anna – at *length* – and we agreed –

Anna Look: I'm sorry, OK? I should have talked to you about it first, sent you an email, put it on a Post-it and stuck it to your door: I, Anna Phillips, am taking a temporary recess from any and all medication.
I just didn't want you to say something perfectly reasonable like . . .
Go on. I know you want to . . .

Silence.

Vivienne This is a safe place for you, Anna. I have always tried to make this is a safe place for you –

Anna I know –

Vivienne So why didn't you feel you could come to me?

Pause.

Anna Things are different now.

Vivienne How so?

Anna I'm eighteen. I've stopped growing. All my life, I've been going forwards, and now I'm here – top of the mountain. The energy I once had to grow bones is now used to break things down.

Vivienne That's a bit morbid.

Anna No, it's a good thing. Because once you realise that all of this previously helpful energy is now aiding your departure from life, you start taking better care of yourself. I've got a gym membership now. I'm reading the backs of cereal boxes. And then I started thinking how strange it was to know the calorie intake of a bowl of cereal, but not the contents of my own medication – don't you think that's strange?

Beat.

Vivienne I have never hidden anything from you, Anna –

Anna That's not what I was –

Vivienne There are certain conversations that you cannot have with an eleven-year-old –

Anna But I'm not eleven years old any more, so –

Vivienne So what would you like to know?

Beat.

Anna The pills – how do they work?

Vivienne Which one?

Anna pulls a few boxes from her bag and studies them.

Anna This one. Start with this one.

Vivienne OK. Quetiapine is an anti-psychotic, which means that it –

Anna – stops me from going all – (*Gestures 'up and down'.*)

Vivienne Yes, and it's thought to work by –

Anna You don't know?

Vivienne We have a reasonably good idea –

Anna Reasonably?

48

Vivienne An informed understanding –

Anna Based on?

Vivienne Anna.

Anna motions to 'go ahead'.

One theory – the most popular theory – is that anti-psychotics reduce the level of dopamine in the brain.

Anna Dopamine . . .

Vivienne It's a kind of chemical messenger. It carries information along the pathways of the brain until it reaches a receptor, and if too much information is absorbed here, you'll start to experience some very unusual thinking.

Anna Like what?

Vivienne Uncommon connections – bizarre associations –

Anna A ten.

Vivienne Yes, 'a ten'. The drug prevents that from happening by blocking the receptors.

Anna And how does the drug know to target *just* the dopamine receptors and nothing else?

Vivienne It doesn't work that way –

Anna So it affects everything?

Vivienne It affects some things we'd prefer it didn't – which is why most people experience side-effects – but there is *a lot* of specificity. It doesn't have an impact on anything relating to your breathing for instance, or appetite control –

Anna What about my ability to write?

—

In order to write a story, you need to be stimulated to do so. You might see something, hear something, remember something – which sets off a whole train of other thoughts – uncommon connections – bizarre associations – a kind of unusual thinking, right?

Vivienne You could call it that, yes.

Anna A pretty intense flow of information –

Vivienne Anna –

Anna – which would require a lot of dopamine, but if the receptors are *blocked* –

Vivienne It's much more complicated than that –

Anna But is it possible? (*Indicating the other pill packets.*) Is it possible one of these, or all of these, made it harder to –

Vivienne There could be some effect, yes.

Pause.

Anna Every day, I wake up, I open up my notebook and . . . nothing. There's nothing! It's like trying to light a match, except you're standing in the wind, or the rain, or you have these really fat-fucking-fingers that can't hold on to the little stick, you know? So you just keep dropping it, over and over again, and it's not because I'm stupid or or or slow, it's because the drugs took my receptors, it blocked them all up; and now that I'm not taking them –

Vivienne You'll start to become very unwell.

Anna But if I can write again –

Vivienne Do you think it will be any easier to write in the midst of a full-blown depression, Anna?

Anna I don't know. I've never tried it.

Beat.

Please, Vivi. I have been on those pills so long, I don't know who I am without them – if the things I say or do are because of the medication or in spite of it – but what I do know is that before you put me on them I could *write*. It's the only thing I know about myself that is true, or real, or in any way authentic – and I was . . . I was *good*. Better than good – I've been thinking for a while now that maybe I could have been, or might have been, or am, or was, some kind of – I don't know – some kind of –

She stops suddenly, worried she might be coming across as unwell.

Vivienne What? Some kind of what?

Anna I don't want to say.

Vivienne Why not?

Anna Because you'll make it something bad – you'll tell me it's something bad –

Vivienne You think you might have been some kind of prodigy?

—

That's a very big thought, Anna.

Anna But what if it's true?

Oliver (*reading*) 'No matter what they tried, Douglas wouldn't stop eating. He ate everything in the cupboards and everything in the fridge, and when his parents locked the kitchen door, he ate the buttons on his clothes and the leather on his shoes, until he was so big they had to roll him from room to room.

'One day, they accidentally rolled him over a piece of broken glass, and Douglas exploded like a balloon, and some of him got caught in a nearby tree, and some of him

51

landed in the neighbour's hedge, but the bottom half of him was carried away by a pack of ravenous seagulls, who fought over his feet, and swallowed his toes, and then pooped him out on beach promenades all over the country.

'His mother gathered what was left of him and ran the pieces through her sewing machine, and his father stuffed him with spare-bedroom pillows, and together they mounted him on the wall, next to a picture of his great-great-grandmother and a painting of a bowl of fruit, and mostly they used him for decoration, but sometimes they hung coats on his ears and hats on his nose, and when guests visited they patted his face and cried "Poor Douglas" before placing their coats on him also.'

Anna Not scared of heights then?

Oliver No, not really.

Anna Good. Because if you fell from here, you wouldn't make it. Twenty feet is all it takes, did you know that? Anything above twenty and cat instincts are useless. I looked it up once, looked up how to survive if you fell from a plane, or if your parachute doesn't open up, or if you slip from scaffolding attached to the side of a building, looked it up and you know what it said? 'It is always best not to fall at all.' That's it! 'It is always best not to fall at all.'

What happens to the body, do you think? The physics of it, not the boring otherworldly stuff. What happens to a body when it falls, all the way, all the way to the ground, what happens to a body when it –

Oliver Rather not think about it, if I'm honest.

Beat.

Anna Sorry . . . Am I doing that thing where I'm talking too much again?

Oliver No, you're fine –

Anna Because I don't *have* to talk. I mean, if you don't want me to talk, I'm happy to just sit here, look at the view –

Oliver No, I like listening to you –

Anna Because it doesn't really seem like it, to be honest –

Oliver No, I promise you, I do – I'd just rather you talk about something that doesn't involve, like –

Anna The total obliteration of a person –

Oliver Yeah.

   Beat.

Anna Want to know the number one reason museums don't have more dinosaur bones?

Oliver Sure. OK.

Anna Car parks.

Oliver Car parks?

Anna I'm serious: there's a whole nether world under there, and people can't get to it any more because we've cauterised it with pipes and concrete slabs. If I could, I'd get one of those digging machines – you know the ones they use to make the Tube? – I'd get one of them, I'd drive it to the nearest Tesco and then I'd dig – down down down – past the ash of the Great Fire and the bodies of a killer plague, past the buckles of a Norman king and the hull of a Viking boat, and then I'd break through the frost from the last ice age and nestle between the bones of a stegosaurus – don't you think that sounds nice?

Oliver Sounds fucking brilliant, yeah.

A comfortable silence. Oliver pulls a notebook out of his bag and hands it to Anna.

I finished it this morning.

—

They're good. I mean, for a kid, they're pretty fucking excellent.

Anna You think so?

Oliver My favourite was the kid who exploded, and then his parents sewed him back together and hung him on the wall as a –

Anna – coat rack.

Oliver Yeah. (*He laughs to himself.*)

Anna My mum thinks they're terrifying.

Oliver Nooo. (*Beat*) Well, maybe a bit. But you were – I dunno – you were smart for your age, so . . .

Anna So?

Oliver *Sooo* . . . maybe you just . . . I dunno . . . maybe you just clued into a few things before the rest of us.

Anna Like what?

Oliver Like the fact that everything is actually a bit shit? I mean, not everything – some stuff is pretty great – but none of it actually means anything, does it? Because no matter what you've achieved, or haven't achieved, or done, or haven't done, one day – for no reason whatsoever – you could fall, or drown, or crash –

Anna Or get eaten by a pack of ravenous seagulls –

Oliver Exactly!

He grins at her.

So. How crazy were you?

Anna Excuse me?

Oliver *Girl Interrupted* crazy or *Fatal Attraction* crazy?

Anna I don't even know what that means.

Oliver Like on a scale of misunderstood teenager to boiling your pet rabbit – where did you fall?

Anna I don't think they use that scale when you're eleven.

Oliver What did you do then? I mean – apart from killing a bunch of imaginary people – what did you actually do?

Anna I don't know. I barely remember any of it.

Oliver How come you have to keep it a secret?

Anna I don't.

Oliver But you don't like telling anyone about it –

Anna Well, yeah . . .

Oliver Why's that?

Anna In case people make bad jokes with shit movie references.

Oliver grins: 'Fair point.'

Do you remember Ashley Becks?

Oliver Kind of?

Anna When I was twelve, I went to a sleepover at Ashley's house. I had a lot of medication to take with me so Mum sorted it out into these cute little pillboxes – she let me decorate it with those awful stick-on earrings, remember those? – stars and crescent moons and hearts – except when I got there I realised all the pills had fallen out in my bag. I didn't know what to do, so I asked

55

Ashley's mum if she could help. I gave her the list of my conditions and what I needed to take for them, and the look on her face . . .

Four weeks later, Izzy had a sleepover and I didn't get an invite. When I asked her why, she told me it was because her mum said that I was a 'risk'. I didn't know what that meant, but Mum did, and when she'd finished screaming at Izzy's mum and then Ashley's mum, she sat me down and gave me a little talk about how lucky I was to have pills for this illness when other people don't have pills for 'stupid'.

Oliver That's rough.

Anna Yeah. Wish she'd just left it alone.

Oliver Your mum? She was brilliant.

Anna She was an idiot. Not like I was overwhelmed with invites after that.

Oliver But you're OK now, right?

Anna What?

Oliver Like, you're not still . . .

Anna No! No, of course not – it was all a really long time ago, so . . .

Oliver So that's all . . .

Anna Yeah, like, I'm actually completely OK now –

Oliver Great! I mean, not 'great', just that I'm glad you're . . . you know . . . I'm glad you're OK.

   Pause.

Anna Year Three or Four?

Oliver Huh?

Anna Mum. When did you have her?

Oliver Four.

Anna Ha. I got out of that one – teacher's kid and all. Had Mr Peters instead. You obviously weren't so lucky.

Oliver She was alright.

Anna Yeah, I'm sure she was!

Oliver No, I'm serious: she was, um . . . she was pretty great, actually. I think my mum had already left by that point so I had to start walking to school – and it was only a mile away so not that big a deal or anything – but one day I got one of those serious after-school detentions for telling Melissa Keane she had too many freckles on her face – which I had no idea was a mean thing to do – because to me it was just like . . . a *fact*, you know? – and by the time I got out it was already dark, and your mum saw me walking home so she stopped the car to give me a lift – but I didn't want anyone to see me riding around in the front seat of my teacher's car, so I just kind of . . . I sat really low like this . . . kept covering my face with my backpack . . . and your mum saw what I was doing – turned it into this giant game – pretended I was a stowaway – like a soldier, or a spy – and she was a secret agent who needed to smuggle me across enemy lines and –

He notices Anna is distracted.

Yeah, OK, sorry if I'm boring you –

Anna No –

Oliver It's stupid, I know.

Anna No, no, it's just . . . (*Beat.*) Sorry. I can't imagine her doing something like that.

Oliver Well, she did, so –

Anna OK, and that's great, but –

Oliver What?

Anna Nothing. It's a nice story.

Silence.

Can I stay at yours tonight?

Oliver What?

Anna Can I stay at yours? For like, a night, or . . . maybe a couple of days, or –

Oliver Why would you want to do that?

Anna I dunno. You always come to mine – and things are a bit weird at the moment with Mum – and it'd be nice to have a break to be honest, and I haven't even seen your place yet – seems a bit unfair that you always stay at mine when I never stay at yours, so . . .

Beat.

You don't want me there, do you?

Oliver Not really, no.

Beat.

Anna Look, I know what I told you is kind of a lot to take in, but I'm fine now, I told you I'm fine –

Oliver Yeah, and I get that –

Anna So when you asked me – when you asked me: 'Why don't you like telling anyone about it?' / Well, this is exactly the reason why! / This is exactly what happens! People stop seeing you as a person, / and they start seeing you as this *thing*, this thing to be managed and –

Oliver Jesus – Anna / Would you just – / I don't want you to come back to mine because I don't want *anyone* to come back to mine, not even my fucking girlfriend, OK?

Beat. Anna smiles.

What?

Anna continues to beam.

Anna – what? Why are you looking at me like that?

Anna Am I your girlfriend?

Oliver What? I dunno.

Anna But you said –

Oliver Yeah, and I didn't mean to, OK?

Anna OK . . . because we've only been seeing each other for like two weeks, so –

Oliver And I'm feeling really fucking embarrassed about that so could you just – I dunno – forget it?

Anna Forget it?

Oliver Change the subject or something – I don't care.

  Beat.

Anna Want to know the dominant colour of the entire universe? (*Beat.*) I mean: if you could exit the universe and see the whole thing out the back window of your space vehicle, do you want to know colour it would be?

Oliver OK.

Anna Beige.

Oliver Beige?

Anna I'm serious! Imagine, for whatever reason, you've travelled a few million years to the edge of the universe, you take out your space camera, you turn around to take the ultimate 'I was here' photo with 200,000 billion observable galaxies in the background, and what does it look like? Horribly, overwhelmingly –

———————————

Renee You're up late.
  —

Did you just get here?

—

I went to bed at eleven. I didn't think you were in the house before then. I could be wrong of course.

—

Oliver, when someone speaks to you –

Oliver I'm just in my boxers, so . . .

Renee I realise that, yes.

Oliver I had to go to the bathroom.

—

I'm just explaining: if I'd known you were out here, I would have put some trousers on.

—

I might do that now, actually –

Renee Would you like to come over for dinner sometime?

Oliver Sorry?

Renee Dinner. I'm inviting you.

—

Come on, Oliver: I'm offering to feed you, not serve you up as main course.

Oliver OK.

Renee Really?

Oliver Yeah, that'd be nice, yeah.

Renee Great.

Oliver I mean, if it's OK with Anna.

Renee Why wouldn't it be?

—

You must think I'm a complete ogre –

Oliver Nooo –

Renee Interrupting the two of you, when you were . . . /
you know . . .

Oliver It's fine.

Renee I didn't mean to get so snappy, but she has this
way of –

Oliver Yeah, I know.

　Beat.

Renee I couldn't sleep. That's why I'm up. I couldn't
sleep.

　—

　How's it going with Anna, anyway?

Oliver Pretty great, actually.

Renee Are you guys 'together' now?

Oliver I think so . . . (*Beat.*) Is that a . . . is that a
problem?

Renee No, God, no – the opposite. I was just thinking
how wonderful that sounds: Anna . . . with *a boyfriend*.
Not that I didn't think she'd ever have one, of course
she'd have one, eventually, I just thought it might take a
special kind of person to . . . (*Beat.*) You may have
noticed that Anna can be a little bit –

Oliver I think she's pretty great, so.

　Beat.

Renee Yes, she is, isn't she? (*Smiles at him.*) I think so
too.

　—

　So . . . what are you doing with yourself now?

Oliver I have a job – an apprenticeship, actually.

Renee Good for you.

Oliver I'm training to be a locksmith – I know that's not exciting or anything – but my dad has this one uncle who's always kind of looked out for me, and he has a shop in town – and I didn't really know what else I should be doing, so . . .

Renee That's sounds great.

Oliver It's just a job.

Renee At least you have one. I have this one daughter, Anna – you might have met her. Lately she's decided she doesn't believe in the 'idea' of a job. I didn't even know a job could be 'an idea', but apparently it is – apparently it's a social construct separating man- and womankind from fulfilling their natural potential – Did you know that, Oliver?

Oliver No, I didn't.

Renee Well, now you do.

Oliver grins at her – a brief moment of shared understanding – then motions back towards Anna's bedroom.

Oliver I should probably –

Renee Oliver?

Oliver Yeah?

Renee Is Anna OK?

Oliver What do you mean?

Renee I mean, have you noticed anything unusual? Sudden changes, or . . .

—

It's just that you spend a lot of time with her, Oliver – at least, I *think* you spend a lot of time with her? – I don't really know what she's doing any more – who she's seeing, where she's going – and that's fine – she's an adult now – I completely understand that – I *respect* that – and I want her to be her own person, but . . .

She's stopped keeping track of her moods, Oliver. There's this chart that we usually fill in together – I'd do it for her – but – as I'm sure you're aware – Anna and I aren't exactly the best of friends right now – so I was wondering if maybe you could . . .

It's very simple. There's a mood scale: zero to ten.

Oliver And – what – you want me to get Anna to fill one in?

Renee No, actually – I was hoping *you* would.

—

I understand why she's doing this, Oliver. Really, I do. And if it turns out Anna can manage without the medication, no one will be happier about that fact than me – but to not keep track of it? At all?

Doesn't that strike you as a little dangerous?

—

I would really appreciate your help.

———————————

Anna My eye won't stop.

There's this twitch in the corner here, won't let up. My hands are always shaking and my heart is just – Can you feel it?

Vivienne moves her hand to Anna's chest.

Supernatural, right?

Vivienne I'm really worried about this, Anna –

Anna But it's not bad, it's not . . . it's not unbearable or anything . . . It's just – (*Staring at her hands, fascinated.*) It's new, isn't it?

63

She continues to pace.

Vivienne Anna – look at me. If someone needs to take medication, it does not make them deficient, weak or in any way less authentic. You are still you – your medication does not change who you are –

Anna – it is the 'Great Emancipator' that lifts the child out of their torment and into a more productive life.

—

I read your book. I was trying to find some information online – your name kept coming up in the search results. I knew you were a big deal, but I didn't realise you were quite so . . .

People really look up to you, don't they?

Vivienne You could say that, yes.

Anna So it's kind of lucky that Mum booked me in to see you so early on. I bet your waiting list now is like . . . out of this world.

Vivienne It's long, but I wouldn't call it quite as long as that.

Anna Are you expensive?

Vivienne Sometimes.

Anna What do you mean, 'sometimes'?

Vivienne I'm paid by the university, not a hospital or a particular clinic. I've taken on patients privately in the past, but now I deal mostly with NHS patients – exceptional or complex cases –

Anna Like Meredith?

Vivienne Meredith?

Anna takes Vivienne's book out of her backpack. She's tabbed several places. She flicks to one of these and begins reading:

'Meredith, for instance, was always ahead of her time. She was talking by eight months, speaking in complete sentences by a year, and writing short novels by the time she entered Junior School. These stories – whilst impressive in size – are dominated by distressing images, revealing the preoccupation with death and separation that is typical of this disorder. Despite this, Meredith's mother, Abby, came up against strong opposition from friends, family and teachers when she suggested that Meredith might benefit from psychiatric help. To convince them, Abby was forced to record one of Meredith's violent rages – in which Meredith can be heard shouting, spitting and swearing, with audible attempts to break the household furniture. "How else," said Abby, "could I possibly explain the terror of living with a child like this?"'

Silence.

Why'd you pick the name Meredith?

Vivienne Meredith is not you, Anna.

Anna She sounds like me –

Vivienne She's not. Meredith, Jack, Sophie, Omar, Emily – these are not just pseudonyms, they're composites, amalgamations of different children I've seen. I promise you – your identity, like those of the other children, was protected at all times –

Anna Is that why you didn't put a name next to any of the stories?

Beat.

You've taken little extracts from stories – put them under each of the chapter headings – That was a nice touch – (*Turning to the front cover.*) It really helps to balance 'groundbreaking clinical research with moving personal

accounts' – only you don't say who wrote them, you say –
a nine-year-old boy, a five-year-old girl, an eleven-year-old girl, a ten-year-old boy – but I wrote them all –

Vivienne Not all of them –

Anna The best ones –

Vivienne But not all of them. Not even half.

Anna Kind of ironic though, isn't it? I've been struggling
for weeks to put a coherent sentence together when here
I am . . . (*Indicating the book.*) Already published.

Pause.

Vivienne Anna . . . there are a lot of people out there
who don't think that this illness exists in children.

Anna Why not?

Vivienne Because they don't know enough about it.
Because they think it must be the parents or the
environment. But mostly, I think, because they're a little
bit frightened of it.
    I wrote this book to change that, Anna – I wrote this
book to change things for *you* –

Anna My dad had just died.

Beat.

You didn't explain that part.
    My dad was walking home from work, when a
complete stranger lost control of her car, and pinned him
up against someone's garden wall. And fifteen minutes
later, he died there, still stuck between the car and the
wall. And everyone kept giving me these really stupid
explanations that mostly involved this, like . . . triumphant
ascent to heaven . . . But someone left a newspaper out,
and I knew how to read, so . . .

And my mother? She refused to leave the house, or eat, or shower, for like . . . months. She couldn't really take care of me, so for a while there my life was this revolving door of aunts and uncles and grandmas and grandpas who came over to do it for her, and I'm no expert on this kind of thing, I know I haven't studied it like you have, but I would call that a possibly traumatic definitely disruptive formative incident that may, or may not, cause some of the symptoms you describe here.

—

Do you know how many drugs I've been on, Vivi?

Vivienne I'd have to check my –

Anna Six. I wrote the list up this morning.
  The first one I couldn't get out of bed, so you swapped it for something that had me bouncing off the walls, but it also made me so fat I didn't want to leave the house. You countered that with the pill that made my hands shake and then swapped that for something that made me nauseous for the whole four months it took me to adjust to it, and then my vision started blurring so you lowered that one, but I wasn't sleeping again, and I started getting these really bad nightmares, so you added something for the insomnia and something for the anxiety, and I have to ask this, Vivi, and I'm sorry, because this question does seem so blindingly obvious: did you ever think that maybe the reason this course of treatment was so ineffective is because your original diagnosis was actually incorrect?

  Silence.

Vivienne I completely understand if want another opinion, Anna. I'm the only doctor you currently have to talk to; I know you'll feel better if you hear it from someone else.

I'd like to refer you to a colleague of mine, Dr Bolton –

Anna Dr Bolton?

Vivienne Do you know who he is?

Anna Chubby guy. No hair. Perfect skin.

Vivienne He's also an excellent adult psychiatrist.

Anna He looks like a giant foetus.

Vivienne Is that an issue for you?

Anna Yes.

Vivienne I can refer you to someone less embryonic if you like?

Anna No.

Vivienne So you'll see Dr Bolton then?

Anna I don't want to see anyone!

—

Why didn't you ask me? Why didn't you ask if you could use my stories?

Vivienne You were eleven years old, Anna; if you'd given permission, it wouldn't have been legally binding –

Anna So you just took them –

Vivienne Of course I didn't. I asked your mother. She gave permission on your behalf.

Silence.

Anna Is this still a safe space for me?

Vivienne Yes. Yes, of course it is.

Anna And I can say anything here?

Vivienne Anything at all.

Anna Because you want me to be honest with you – you always say that – 'Anna, I want you to be completely honest with me.'

Vivienne And I do. I still do.

Anna OK. Because that name you chose . . . *Meredith*? I fucking *hate* that name.

Renee How's the quiche, Oliver?

Oliver It's good, yeah.

Renee You haven't started.

Oliver I have.

Renee You haven't really touched it though.

Oliver No, no, I have.

Renee You've pulled the bacon out of it.

Oliver It was really great bacon.

Renee You don't want to try the rest of it?

Oliver I'm just, uh –

Renee What?

Oliver I'm just taking my time.

Renee Anna, you're not hungry either?
—
You don't feel like talking, Anna?

Oliver Anna.
Anna.

Renee motions for him to back down.

Renee So. Oliver. What did you get up to today?

69

Oliver Not much. Slept till three.

Renee You didn't have work?

Oliver I got two call-outs last night.

Renee Oh no, I'm so sorry.

Oliver No, no, it's a good thing. If I get a call after midnight, the pay doubles.

Renee Well, that *is* good. I mean, not for the poor people who got locked out of their houses, but very good for you.

Oliver I guess it is, yeah! (*Between mouthfuls*) What about you? How was school?

Renee Well . . . halfway through term and I've already implemented a seating plan . . .

Oliver That bad, huh?

Renee Oh, Oliver . . . much *much* worse. (*Leaning in.*) You know, most of the time, my battle strategy is to pick out the troublemakers – slot each of them alongside the better-behaved kids – but lately I've been thinking: why punish the good kids? So today I decided to make all the really obnoxious ones sit around the same table for a week. My hope is that their understanding of the universe will evolve to encompass more than one person, but I suppose there's always that risk they'll close ranks and . . . I don't know . . . stage an uprising or something. It hasn't happened yet, but I know it's coming . . .

Oliver You ever force me to sit anywhere?

Renee Why would I do that?

Oliver I dunno.

Renee You were such a lovely kid, Oliver.

Oliver Noo –

Renee No, you were. You were such a lovely little –

Anna I've been doing a lot of research lately.

   Beat.

Renee Oh?

Anna Quite a bit of it actually.

Renee Good for you, Anna. Glad you're keeping yourself busy.

Anna There's this video online that you might find interesting. It's from an international psychiatry conference and Vivienne is one of the speakers –

Renee Why don't you email me the link? I'll watch it later.

Anna No, it's OK. I can tell you about it now.

Renee Let's talk about it later.

Anna I want to talk about it now.

Renee I don't think it's appropriate dinner conversation.

Anna It's very appropriate.

Renee We have a guest, Anna.

Anna It's Oliver.

Renee Oliver is our guest.

Anna You feed him every night – at what point can we dock his privileges?

Renee Don't talk about people as if they're not in the room, Anna.

   Beat. Anna turns to Oliver.

Anna Oliver, do you mind me talking about this very interesting thing I watched on the internet today?

Oliver Um . . . I guess not?

Anna Great. As I was saying, there's this video online that you might find interesting. It's from an international psychiatry conference, and Vivienne is one of the speakers –

Renee Yes, we got that part –

Anna And not just this conference – lots of conferences – Madrid, Milan, Melbourne, Chicago, Berlin, New York, New Delhi – for a clinical researcher salaried to the one university, Vivienne is surprisingly well-travelled.

Beat.

Renee That's very interesting, Anna. Thank you for sharing that –

Anna But the thing is, Mother, the reason Vivienne's so popular, the reason everyone wants her to speak at their conferences – and this is just my personal opinion, by the way – but the reason that everyone wants her to speak at their conferences is because unlike the other presenters – Vivienne actually knows how to tell a story. And I don't mean that in the figurative sense like, 'Oh God, that speech really took me on a journey' – I mean, she reads an *actual* story. (*Beat.*) She didn't write them of course – that much is obvious – but she's incredibly good at reading them – and the two or three hundred people listening to her at any one time, they just . . . they *love* it.

Beat.

Renee Well. I'm really pleased to hear that, Anna –

Anna Pleased?

Renee If Vivienne's book is having that kind of impact, then think of all the young people who are now getting the help that they need.

She returns to her food. Anna stares at her.

Anna Did you used to hide my medication in my food –

Renee (*under her breath*) Jesus, Anna–

Anna (*flipping through Vivienne's book*) Did you ever record one my tantrums and show it to your friends?

Renee How are the beans, Oliver?

Anna / Are you the one who lost her temper and / shovelled dinner into her kid's mouth? / Did you ever change the clocks just to get me to go to bed earlier?

Oliver / The beans?

Renee / The long green things stacked on the side of your plate.

Oliver I know what beans are.

Anna Mum.

Renee I cooked them with butter and garlic.

Anna Mum.

Renee So they're not just vegetables –

Oliver They look like vegetables –

Anna Mum.

Renee They *are* vegetables, but they've been cooked in a way that makes them seem less terrifying.

Anna Mum, did you hear what I said?

Renee Yes, Anna.

Anna So why didn't you answer my question?

73

Renee I'm choosing to ignore it.

Anna Why?

Renee Because this is the illness talking and not you. (*To Oliver.*) How was the rest of your day?

Anna / The illness?!

Oliver Fine, thanks.

Renee (*to Oliver*) Did you get up to anything else?

Anna It's not some fucking separate entity.

Renee Language, Anna.

Anna It's not some fucking separate entity. It's not some spirit taking possession. You're my mother, not Mystic-fucking-Meg –

Oliver Anna!

Renee (*to Oliver*) It's fine –

Oliver (*to Renee*) She shouldn't talk to you that way.

Renee Oliver, please –

Oliver I was just defending you –

Renee And that's very admirable, but I think we should all just . . . (*Pause. A breath.*)

   Oliver goes back to his food. Anna stares at him.

Oliver What?
—
Stop it, Anna.
—
What?!

Anna Do you want to know the only reason you're here, Oliver?

   I said: do you want to know the only reason you're here? The only reason Mum has you round so often?

Oliver No, not really –

Anna It's so you can take care of me. It's true. She thinks you're level-headed. Straightforward. *Unaffected.* Just like her. And she's happy about that because now she has someone to pass all that responsibility on to. Isn't that right, Mum?

    Renee ignores her.

Mum.
   Mum.
   Mum.

Renee Yes, Anna?

Anna Do you want to know the only reason Oliver's here?

Renee No doubt you'll tell me anyway.

    Oliver and Renee wait for the response. Anna doesn't say anything.

(*To Oliver.*) How long do you have left?

Oliver Sorry?

Renee Of the apprenticeship? How long do you have left?

Oliver 'Bout a week.

Renee Gosh – that's crept up!

Oliver I guess so, yeah.

Renee And then what: do they keep you on, do you get your own shop?

Oliver I dunno yet. I think they'll keep me on; my own shop would be cool though. My own van. I'd like that, yeah –

Anna Food, mostly.

    Beat.

Renee Sorry Anna?

Anna He's here for the food, mostly. There are lots of other reasons, of course, but they all run along a similar theme.

Renee Maybe you can share those some other time –

Anna His place has no washing machine. It's never had one. Oliver was washing his clothes in the kitchen sink until I taught him how to use the washing machine here. And now that he no longer uses the sink to wash his clothes, it's disappeared – poof! – right under a pile of plates. Plates on the floor. Food on the floor. Rats too, I'm guessing. Not Oliver's fault of course. It's that shiftless father you have.

Oliver He's disabled.

Anna He's fat, Oliver. He's a fat old man stuck in a chair so long he's become part of it.

Renee Anna!

Anna I just think it's disrespectful to people in wheelchairs when Oliver's dad lost the use of his legs through inactivity alone.

Renee ENOUGH.

Anna I'm not done yet.

Renee You most certainly are.

Anna I'm not, actually –

Renee Anna, if you don't shut it right now –

Anna What? What will you do, Mother?

Renee chooses to say nothing.

As I was saying, Oliver, when you add up all the positives of dating me, you realise how little I actually factor into the equation. And it's nothing to be embarrassed about. Really, it's not; all men crave maternal affirmation. But see, *that's* what I find so amusing about this whole situation – because here we have Oliver – who wants someone to take care of him – and there we have Renee – who wants a care*taker*. So really, no one in this situation is ever going to get anything they want, because you're both after something completely different.

That's funny when you think about it. Isn't that funny?

Renee What Anna is forgetting, Oliver, is that this is my house, not hers, and you are welcome in it any time you like.

Anna You know, I realised something just now –

Renee throws her hands up in disbelief.

I realised that Oliver and I are both half-orphans.

Renee (*clearing plates*) Let's have some dessert. Do you want some dessert, Oliver?

Oliver That'd be great, thanks.

Anna I mean: I know you're not really a half-orphan.

Renee Anna. Would you like some dessert?

Anna No, thank you. (*To Oliver.*) I know you're not really a half-orphan. I know, *technically*, you still have two parents. But for the purposes of this argument, let's say you have one.

Renee exits with the plates.

Because having one parent, instead of two, significantly damages the child. And it's not because there's a lack of either female- or male-specific influence in the child's life, it's because there's no *discussion* regarding the raising of that child. Single parenthood, by definition, is an autocracy. No one else to say: 'Hey, that's not a good idea. Don't do that.' Do you understand what I'm saying, Oliver? There's no one else to do that.

Did you know I was my father's favourite?

Oliver You're an only child.

Renee re-enters with dessert.

Anna No, I mean in the family, I was my father's favourite. In the family. Between the three of us there was a clear hierarchy of needs, and he always put mine first. He was great fun, my dad. And he loved my stories. I'd leave one out half finished and by the next morning it would be done. 'Midnight fairies' he used to blame it on. Isn't that nice? He was a brilliant man, my dad. (*As Dad.*) 'Leave her alone, Renee. Kids should be kids.' He used to put his napkin over his head like this and talk to me through the hole.

She punctures a hole in the paper napkin, pushes her lips through it and affects a cartoon-like voice.

'Hello, Anna. Hello. You'll have to feed me tonight, Anna. I seem to have misplaced my eyes.'

Oliver (*indicating the dessert*) This is really good, Renee.

Renee Thanks, love.

Anna Makes you wonder, doesn't it? What things would have been like if he was here now? Makes you wonder.

Renee Are you staying tonight, Oliver?

Oliver No, I don't think so.

Renee Would you like me to drive you home?

Oliver That'd be great, thanks.

Renee What time will we be seeing you tomorrow?

Anna Right before dinner's ready, I imagine.

Renee How much longer do we have to put up with this?

—

Answer me, Anna. How much longer is this going to last?

—

I *understand* that today is not a good day for you, and I *recognise* that it's sometimes difficult for you to control the things that you say and the things that you do, but please, for one moment, consider the effect that this 'personal experiment' of yours is having on the rest of us –

Anna Personal experiment?

Renee That's what it is, isn't it?

—

Oliver and I have been talking –

Oliver Renee –

Renee Oliver and I have been talking and we think it's time you went back on your medication.

—

We've been tracking your moods over the past couple of weeks and –

Anna I'm sorry, what?

Renee We've been tracking your moods over the past couple of weeks, and we think it's fairly evident that –

Anna Oh my God . . . (*She laughs to herself.*)

Renee Oliver, would you like to say something?

Oliver No, not really.

Renee I think now would be a good time to say something.

Pause.

Oliver It's not always easy to –

Renee To Anna. You need to say it to Anna.

Beat.

Oliver It's not always easy to, um . . . be around you. And I think it's getting worse, because when we first got together, you were so . . . and now you're . . . not . . . and it doesn't look like it's getting any better, so . . . don't you think it's time to see your doctor again?

Anna moves to leave.

Renee Where are you going? Don't even think about leaving the house in that mood.

Anna Bed. I'm going to bed.

Renee Yes. I think that's probably a good idea.

Anna stares at Oliver. Oliver stares at his plate.

Maybe we can continue this discussion tomorrow?

Anna exits.
Renee and Oliver continue to eat in silence.

Oliver You shouldn't let her get away with that.

Renee She's not well, Oliver; you know that.

A long silence.

I should go check on her. Make sure she's actually in bed, not halfway down the street –

Oliver She'll be fine.

Renee I should check though.

Oliver She's probably just sitting there. Sulking. She does that a lot.

Renee Yes, she does.

Oliver It's weird.

Renee I'll go check on her –

Anna returns clutching a bottle of pills.
Silence.

I thought you were going to bed.

Anna I changed my mind.

She takes out a pill and swallows it.

I tried to go to sleep, I did, but then I couldn't stop thinking about what you both said. And the more I thought about it, the more sense it actually made. You're right. It's selfish of me not to be on medication. It's incredibly thoughtless actually – how could I be so? – I mean: I never even *considered* how my 'personal experiment' might affect the *two of you*.

She takes out another pill, lets it roll around in her hand.

No point carrying on with it, I guess. I've missed quite a few. I should probably catch up.

She swallows the pill.
Renee takes a step towards Anna.
Anna pours four or five more on to her hand.
Renee takes another step towards her and Anna downs them.
Anna pours a dozen more on to her hand.
They stare at each other.
Renee races towards her and Anna shoves them into her mouth and dashes out of the way. She runs to the table, grabs her mother's glass of wine and washes the pills down. Renee reaches her and pins her to the table.

Renee Open your mouth. Open it. OPEN IT.

She forces her own fingers inside. Anna gags and struggles, beats at her mother, swears at her.

Oliver, I need you to call the ambulance please.
Oliver . . .
Oliver!

Oliver pulls out his phone and calls 999.
   Over this, Vivienne enters and reads to an unseen audience.

Oliver (*on the phone*)
Hi – we need a, um . . .
we need an ambulance
. . .

> *Anna pushes her mother off her and tries to leave but Renee scrambles after her, pulls her to the ground – much of the tableware goes with it.*

My, uh . . . my . . . she's swallowed a lot of pills?
. . . I don't . . . I don't know what kind . . .
no, she's, um . . . she's awake . . . she's breathing . . . 24 Hurstbourne Road – yeah – yeah that's it . . .

> *Anna tries to drag herself away – using whatever means she has available – chairs, the rug, sheer*

Vivienne (*reading*) 'We used to fight about it all the time.

'She refused to take them – she'd knock the pills right out of my hand or she'd pretend to swallow them, and then spit them out as soon as she got the chance.

'At first, I used a pill cutter so that I could get the pieces small enough to hide in her food, or I'd grind them down, stir it into her drinks. I had to do this every day for about three months, and then one day, I watch Meredith go to the kitchen bench – where I kept her medications – I watch her go to the kitchen bench, take out the pill packets and count out the correct dose herself – no prompting required.

'I think she could sense the changes – the levelling – the

brute force etc. Renee grabs
her and holds her down.

OK, I'll, um – do I hang up
or – OK, no, no, I can stay,
that's fine – how long until
they, um – OK . . .

Oliver steps quietly into
the background and looks
elsewhere, unable to
watch.

calm. I think she knew
that the illness was
retreating – that this
prison around her mind
was breaking down – and
that she was becoming
more of herself.

'And that moment was
the first time in three . . .
maybe four years . . . that
I allowed myself to think
. . . everything is going to
be OK . . . everything is
actually going to be OK.'

Blackout.

End of Act One.

Act Two

Renee (*reading*) 'The thing that scared her most was not hiding in a cupboard, or under the bed, or floating in the corners of the room like a ghost. The thing that scared her most was inside her head, pressing its thumbs against the backs of her eyeballs and whispering from the insides of her ears: "You have been chosen, not for one unhappiness, but hundreds, and I will make you yell at your mother, and hit your friends, and bite and scrape and burn your own skin, I will make the days long and the nights even worse, and you will hide in your bed, under the blankets, and in the dark, away from the lights and the crowds and the noise, until the day you decide that things would be easier if you never woke up at all."'

———————————

Anna If I have to stay here, I want my own room.

Vivienne They don't have any private rooms here.

Anna Broke my arm once. Had my own room then.

Vivienne Perhaps you were at a different hospital.

Anna So where do I request an upgrade?

Vivienne This isn't a hotel, Anna.

Anna No, it's a floor full of old people: sixteen beds and a person dying in each one of them! It's not good for the soul to be around that. It's not good for me – right now – to be around that.

Vivienne I know what you're doing.

84

Anna What am I doing?

Vivienne That kind of thing might work on your mother, but it won't work on me.

Anna I have no idea what you're talking about.

Vivienne What you did last night was cruel and stupid.

Anna That's a dangerous thing to say to someone on the brink of despair.

Vivienne You are the smartest person I know, Anna Phillips. If you'd wanted to kill yourself, you would have worked out exactly how to do so. Instead you took the one drug on your prescription that is impossible to overdose on. You know this, and I know you know this because I told you.

  Silence.

Anna Where's Mum?

Vivienne I sent her out to get something to eat.

Anna Where's Oliver?

Vivienne I don't know. Have you tried calling him?

Anna Didn't really have time to pack my phone, so . . .

Vivienne You'll be out soon. You can call him when you get home.

  She collects her things.

Anna Where are you going?

Vivienne You're not the only person I have to see today.

Anna Big night for slashers, was it?

Vivienne That's a horrible word.

Anna It's a great word: it describes the act and simultaneously elicits the horror of performing it. It was

Gen Y's favourite pastime growing up. What's Gen Z up to now? Detergent cocktails? Inhaler burns? Necktie round the bedpost? I forget what the kids are into these days.

Vivienne If you're trying to shock me, it's not working.

Anna I'm not trying to shock you, I'm genuinely interested. How many of your patients are currently in here, Vivienne? Three? Four? And does this kind of thing happen often in your professional life? In nature, how many times must something occur before it's considered *a pattern*? That's all I'm trying to figure out.

Vivienne moves to leave.

I never said I wanted to die.

—

I didn't. I never said that.

—

And I shouldn't have to die, you know, before pain becomes valid. You shouldn't set someone that challenge.

Silence. Vivienne walks back towards Anna.

Vivienne I'd put you in a private room if I could. Unfortunately, the assessment rooms are full and you need to be supervised. This floor was the only one with a bed close to the nurses' station.

Anna I'm high risk, am I?

Vivienne You're the most likely to run away.

Anna That's because I'm the only here who can run.

Vivienne There's that famous sense of humour! Nice to see last night's pill blowout hasn't completely addled the brain –

Anna Do you like me?

—

Do you like me?

86

Vivienne Anna –

Anna You've known me since I was eleven. That's longer than most of my friends. Almost as long as Dad. You've seen me once a month, every month for seven years. Do you like me?

Silence.
Vivienne checks her watch.

Vivienne Has anyone been to see you yet?

—

Someone should have been round to make an assessment.

—

Anna?

Anna Why can't you do it?

Vivienne I don't work here. You'll be seeing someone from the hospital instead.

Anna Lucky me.

Vivienne I can stay if you like – feed them the answers?

Anna No. Thank you.

Vivienne Are you sure? It will make the whole process far less painful . . .

Anna ignores her.

Anna Jean Phillips. Eighteen years old. 'Jean' after the grandmother who used to bake, not after the one who accidentally locked her in the basement. Loves the colour green. Ambivalent about pink. Objects profoundly to the colour blue because it reminds her of the liquid television actors pour into sanitary napkins to demonstrate there's no leakage. She makes me a birthday card every birthday, a Christmas card every Christmas, and she once assured me, age eleven, what a relief it was to speak to someone on her 'intellectual level'. She hates her ears – always asks the hairdresser to leave enough length to cover them – but I suspect she's forgotten how readily she once used them to certify her elfin ancestry. She's broken the same leg twice, her arm once, and, if I'm not mistaken, she should have a sizeable scar on her right hand from the time she slammed her fingers in the car door, age . . . thirteen?

Pause.

It will never be appropriate for you and I to be friends. You do understand that, don't you?

After a few moments, Anna nods.

Would you like to stay on with me, Anna?

Beat.

Anna What do you mean?

Vivienne The rest of your team will change – you'll still move to Adult Services – but I'll continue on as your psychiatrist.

Anna I thought that wasn't allowed –

Vivienne I couldn't tell you in case it wasn't approved, but I asked for special dispensation –

Anna Am I part of your research again?

Pause.

Vivienne That's my job, Anna – it has always been part of my job – I work with patients and I conduct research – each side supports the other –

Anna Is there going to be another book?

Beat.

Vivienne I don't know yet. (*Pause.*) Potentially.

Oliver Renee?

Renee Hello.

Oliver What are you doing here?

Renee Can I come in?

Oliver No.

Renee No?

Oliver It's a mess.

Renee I don't mind.

Oliver My dad's sleeping.

Renee I'll be quiet.

He doesn't move to let her pass.

OK. Fine. You know it's probably going to snow today, but that's fine.

Oliver Let me get you a coat –

Renee I said it's fine.

—

Anna's home now. They only kept her a night, so . . . so she's been home for a while.

—

She's a bit emotional, that's all – hasn't been able to get you on the phone.

—

At first, I was worried that something might have happened to you, but Anna saw a picture of you online – smiling – big pint of beer in your hand –

Oliver I had a work thing.

Renee What kind of work thing?

Oliver Last day of my apprenticeship.

Beat.

Renee Oliver . . .

Oliver Best part is, boss said he'd hire me. And they're going to franchise soon. Might get my own van. My own shop. And I only had a beer, I didn't get drunk or anything, just wanted to be respectful, you know? (*Beat.*) You're not mad, are you?

Renee Mad? Why would I be mad?

Oliver I dunno, seems a bit wrong to be happy when, uh, you know –

Renee Oh come here, you big idiot! Congratulations!

She wraps him up in a big bear hug.

Oliver Alright, steady on. Not that big a deal.

Renee It is! It absolutely is! We should celebrate!

Oliver I can't.

Renee I'm not going to throw you a party, Oliver. Just let me cook you dinner, OK?

Oliver That's really nice, thank you, but I can't.

Renee Of course you can.

Oliver I can't, Renee.

Renee Why? Do you have a better offer?

Oliver sits down suddenly and puts his head in his hands. Almost as soon it starts, he makes a concerted effort to squash whatever it is he is feeling. Renee stares at him uncomfortably.

Oliver? Are you . . .?

Oliver Sorry, I, uh –

Renee It's OK –

Oliver No, it's not, it's not, it's really, uh, it's really embarrassing, and, uh –

Renee Hey, hey, it's fine, it's fine.

She sits down next to him, careful not to intrude on his personal space.

It's a shock seeing her like that, I know.

When she was little, I used to call it 'the volcano effect'. You could see the anger rising up inside of her – everything you and I tend to feel in moderation – she'd feel it all at once, and all of that energy – it has to go somewhere, doesn't it?

But once she was finished, once she had said and done everything she possibly could to make sure I was as miserable as she was, then she'd start coming back again – piece by piece and – oh God! – when Anna is happy, everything is such a joy. Colours are brighter. Food tastes better. If music is on, even in a public place, there is no way in hell you are staying in your seat. The sun isn't bright – it is *dazzling*, do you understand that?

And you should have seen her at the hospital, Oliver. She was so apologetic – genuinely, genuinely ashamed of herself – and she and Vivienne had a long talk about going back on the medication, and now, now she's finally come round to the idea.

So you just . . . just . . . (*Patting his leg.*) Just hang in there, alright? You hang in there, and I'll hang in there, and together we'll steer HMS Anna back in the right direction –

Oliver I'm going to break up with her.
—

Not right now, not when she's . . .

I thought I'd wait a while? Wait till she's better before I tell her. I don't want to lie to her, but I don't want to

91

pretend either, so I, um . . . I thought I might stay away?
I thought that might be best –

Renee For whom?

—

I really hoped you weren't going to do this, Oliver.
I really hoped you were a better person than this –

Oliver Don't say that –

Renee All her life Anna has had people judging her,
judging her for being on her medication, and then
judging her for being off it, and it's just ignorance, that's
all it is, because people make judgements about things
they don't understand –

Oliver You stuck your fingers down her throat!

Beat.

I watched you do that.
  And after that, I watched the paramedics carry her out
of the house, and I'm supposed to be OK with that
because – what? – in a few days the sun will shine a little
brighter?
  And you've been so good to me, Renee, hanging out
with me, talking to me and stuff – and I'm going to miss
that, I am – but it's not enough to . . . I mean, I'm
twenty-one! I have had to take care of people my entire
life, I have had to take care of people who should have
been taking care of *me* – why the *fuck* would I sign up
for one more?
  (*Beat.*) I'm sorry –

Renee It's OK.

Oliver No, I mean it.

Renee It doesn't matter.

Oliver I wouldn't normally swear, but –

Renee I'm sure you swear all the time.

Oliver Yeah I do, but –

Renee So why can't you swear in front of me?
   Am I too old now? Is that it? Have I crossed over some age-related threshold, where some words, some excellent fucking words, are no longer available to me?
   Fuck. Shit. Fucking shit. Fucking shit fuck shit fuck shit fuck shit.
   Your turn.

Oliver What?

Renee Go on.

Oliver Arse.

Renee That's it? That's all you've got?

Oliver Dick.

Renee Better.

Oliver Bitch, bastard, dickhead, shithead, wankstain –

Renee Wankstain?

Oliver It's an insult.

Renee It's brilliant.

Oliver Yeah?

Renee Genius even. So mundane and yet so fucking *brutal*.

   They fall into a comfortable silence.

Don't come to the house.
   Let me get her back on track – give her a week or so to settle on the medication – and then I want you to come and tell her yourself . . . or . . . or don't.
   Don't. That's probably better.

   After a few moments, Oliver extends his hand.

Oliver Best of luck, yeah?

Renee You too, kiddo.

Anna is experiencing a severe depression made worse by the sedative effects of her medication. She's heavy and tired, devoid of any strong emotion, urge or motivation. Days pass, maybe weeks, but any sense of movement is muffled and indistinct as if Anna is watching it all from behind thick glass or several feet under water.

Renee Keys . . . keys . . . Anna, have you seen my keys? (*Spying them*) Gotcha! Alright, I'm off. Mrs Stokes will be here in a few minutes. You remember Mrs Stokes from down the road? She's offered to keep you company for a couple of hours, that'll be nice won't it? Nice of her to offer to do that?

—

She knows as much as she needs to know, and I doubt she hangs out with your lot, so you don't have to worry about all that.

—

What? What is it?

—

Do you want to take a shower? That's fine, love. I'll go give Mrs Stokes the keys. She'll let herself in.

—

What?

—

Come on, Anna, what is it?

Anna I need a razor.

—

For my legs.

—

Please?

94

Renee I'll pay for you to get your legs waxed.

—

Waxing's better, anyhow. They'll be lovely and smooth for longer. Grows back finer, doesn't it?

—

I have to go now.

Anna Mum.

Renee Anna, I have to go.

Anna *Mum.*

Renee What?

She notices the hairbrush in Anna's hand. She puts her bag down and takes a moment to run the brush through Anna's hair.

Why don't you try writing today? Take advantage of some of this time?

—

I bought you something. I was going to wait until your birthday, but I suppose it . . .

—

I'll go get it.

She exits and returns with a wrapped present.

Do you want to open it?

Anna doesn't respond so Renee opens it herself: two books, Jack Kerouac's On the Road *and Jane Austen's* Pride and Prejudice.

Renee Jack and Jane, remember?

—

I thought that might make you laugh.

—

Well, at the very least, you can use it as inspiration. Jane, preferably. Jack drank himself to death in the end, although Jane never left her mother's house. Anyway, I'm sure they're a good read.

Silence as Renee sweeps Anna's hair into a ponytail.

I want you to remember this, Anna. This. What you're feeling now. The next time you consider coming off your medication, I want you to remember how heavy you felt. Will you do that for me? Please?

Pause.

I have to go now.

Anna Don't.

Renee Come on, Anna.

Anna Please . . .

Renee Don't start this again, I *have* to go.

Anna *Please.*

Renee I'll see you tonight.

Anna No . . .

Renee I'm sorry, Anna –

Anna No . . . no . . . NO!

Renee leaves.
   In the silence, Anna can hear everything – water dripping, the gentle hum of the refrigerator, road noise from outside etc.
   Needing a distraction, she picks up her mobile phone and dials Oliver's number. It rings through to voicemail.
   With extreme difficulty:

Anna Hi . . . it's me . . . again . . . obviously. Um . . . Would you . . . would you mind giving me a call back?

I'm sure you . . . have . . . a lot of things you want to say
to me . . . all of which I, uh . . . I probably deserve, and
I . . . I have a lot of things I want to say to you . . . none
of which I, um . . . none of which I really want to leave in
a message, so . . .

Pause.

Do you . . . do you want to know the only word in the
English language that rhymes with 'orange'?

Oliver smiles.

'Sporange'.
    I know that sounds like a . . . like a made-up word . . .
but it's not. It's like this . . . it's like this little knapsack
that uh . . . ferns and moss and algae use to carry all
their, um . . . all their spores around in . . . but I guess it's
not . . . really a word anyone knows except, um . . .
botanists . . . and, um . . . me . . . and now you, so . . .

Anna tries not to cry.

Want to know . . . the only land mammal that doesn't
know . . . how to jump?
    (Mimicking game-show buzzer sound.) Ehh – sorry.
You've um . . . you've reached your . . . quota . . .
today . . . for completely useless pieces of . . . information,
so . . . if you . . . if you want to know the answer . . . you
have to, um . . . you have to call me back.

Anna hangs up, exhausted.
    Oliver fades.
    *The household sounds resume, and Anna closes her
eyes, barring herself against it. She shakes, sweats and
scratches at her arms.*

Renee I was in the area.

—

There was no one at the front desk, so I just sort of –

Beat. She notices the lunch in Vivienne's hand.

I'm sorry, is this a bad time, or –

Vivienne I don't see Anna until the end of the week.

Renee I know. I was hoping that maybe you and I could –

Vivienne If Anna is OK with it, you're more than welcome to attend?

Renee Come on, Viv, you know she doesn't want me there –

Vivienne Then we both need to respect that.

Beat.

Renee She hasn't left the house for three weeks, Viv. Her head aches, her joints hurt – everything is too bright and too loud – she is cycling so rapidly I don't have time to get my breath back – and now she's telling me her skin is crawling? – I've had to cut back her fingernails because she keeps trying to scratch it off – and I expected her to get ill again – I braced myself for that – but this? – what she's experiencing now?
   I don't remember this at all.

Pause.

Vivienne I have ten minutes before my next appointment.

Renee Thank you.

Vivienne And then I really will need to –

Renee No, no, I understand – Thank you.

Vivienne makes some kind of conciliatory gesture towards a chair or the centre of the room.

Vivienne Renee . . . I warned Anna her symptoms could escalate if she came off her medication.

Renee OK . . .

Vivienne Rapid withdrawal from long-term medication will usually cause some kind of relapse –

Renee No, no, I get that – I do – but you don't expect an illness to get *worse* after taking medication, right? You expect it to get better, or you expect it to go back to the same level of difficult-to-manage that it was before, you don't expect it to escalate and you certainly don't expect entirely new symptoms to develop – so why is this happening to her?

Vivienne Anna has been on that medication for seven years, the brain will adapt to that – compensate, even –

Renee Compensate . . .

Vivienne It might become more sensitive. If you stop the drugs – and abruptly, as Anna has done – it's like opening the floodgates – the chemicals are now getting through again, only the brain is absorbing even more of it.

Renee So how long before it stops doing that?

Vivienne It doesn't work like that.

Renee Why not?

Vivienne You can't rewind something as complex as the human brain, Renee –

Renee And what does that mean? The pills have . . . what? . . . *permanently* changed it –

Vivienne *Potentially* changed. It's just a theory to explain why a relapse might be more severe after medication than before – but you also have to allow for the fact that Anna is an adult now and the illness manifests differently in adults –

Renee But which is it?

Vivienne Well, there's no way of knowing –

Renee No way of knowing what? No way of knowing if this is the illness returning, or she's been on the pills for so long she can't cope without them –

Vivienne She couldn't cope before –

Renee Anna thinks otherwise –

Vivienne And if Anna has any concerns about that –

Renee But Anna didn't make the decision to come here – I did!

I was the one who found your contact details. I asked for the referral. I gave you her stories. I told you what I thought they meant. And I filled all those questionnaires in – do you remember those? You gave me a list of her behaviours and I had to circle an answer to indicate how pervasive they were – Never, Always, Sometimes – Never, Always, Sometimes – but more often than not I was circling the word 'Sometimes' – over and over again – *sometimes* she has nightmares, *sometimes* she displays aggressive behaviour towards others, *sometimes* she has exaggerated ideas about herself and her abilities – but within that word 'sometimes' is a vast expanse of other moments when she was perfectly capable, and good, and kind, and the idea that in circling that one word I might have set her off on a course that you are now telling me she *cannot* come back from . . . I don't think I . . . (*Beat.*) I don't think I can cope with being responsible for that.

Silence.

Vivienne I've known Anna a long time now.

Renee You have, yes.

Vivienne And during that time, I've grown to understand her, to care for her, but the first time you brought that little girl in . . . she terrified me. Here was this funny, confident, fiercely intelligent little girl with night terrors, separation anxiety, oppositional behaviour, violent rages and a preoccupation with ending her young life before it had even started.

There are a great many factors that initiated and then exacerbated this illness – some, admittedly, we don't fully understand – so I find it more helpful to focus on the things we *do* know: Anna has had seven years of relative stability. She finished school. She began her first proper relationship – and – until recently, she'd managed to hold down a full-time job. These achievements may not be on the scale that Anna would like them to be, but given her history, they are *extraordinary*.

Anna's medication? It *works*.

Renee Have you ever taken one?

Beat.

For research, for science, out of sheer curiosity, I don't know – have you ever taken one?

Vivienne Have you?

Beat.

Renee Just one.
I wanted to know what it felt like.
Within fifteen minutes, I was so tired I couldn't keep my eyes open. I had to put myself to bed mid-afternoon and then I slept for thirteen hours straight. When Anna was eleven, she was on two of those, a *day* –

Vivienne – which enabled her to function in the world!

Beat.

Renee – you didn't wake up one morning and decide to take your child to a psychiatrist – I wasn't your first point of call, I wasn't even your second or your third.

You tried behavioural therapies, herbal remedies, breathing exercises, diet changes – gluten, lactose, dairy – she didn't eat sugar for a year! And then you saw doctor after doctor after doctor before you finally honoured the idea that your child *might* be suffering from a mental illness – and *then* . . . only then . . . did you come to me.

And I took my time. I got to know her. I weighed up the options – and of course, it would be infinitely easier if I could pick up an X-ray of her brain, point to some black or foggy part of it and say: here – here it is – physical proof! But I can't do that – the mind is a frustratingly intangible thing – so there are a million unknowns – a million different possibilities at play – including a small chance that – as Anna seems to believe – there was absolutely nothing wrong with her to begin with – but the alternative? That your daughter was suffering from a difficult but completely treatable disorder – that she was seriously considering taking her own life – and you and I did . . . what? . . . you and I did nothing to help her . . .?

Pause.

(*Glancing at her watch.*) I'm really sorry, but I have a patient waiting –

Renee I need to talk to someone.

Vivienne I've already explained everything I can –

Renee Not about Anna.

Vivienne Then I don't understand –

Renee *I* need to talk to someone. *Me.* (*Beat.*) I'm not really sleeping at the moment. I have this, uh . . . I have this kind of, uh, it's a bit like a tremor . . . (*Indicates her heart.*) here, and –

Vivienne Renee –

Renee (*gathering her things; embarrassed*) No, no, you're right, you're right – Thank you for your time today –

Vivienne Wait a minute . . .

Renee And you've certainly given me a lot to think about, so –

Vivienne *Renee.*

Renee stops.

Would you mind if I gave you some advice?

She's not a child any more. You won't be able to take care of her like you used to and that is a *good* thing. If Anna is going to become the capable young woman I know you want her to be, then she needs to learn how to manage this illness herself, and that means taking a step back, and not just for her sake – yours too.

You need to take care of yourself, Renee – take a break once in a while –

Renee A break? From Anna?

Vivienne See friends, join the gym, take a spin class, I don't know –

Renee A spin class?

Vivienne Something . . . something that has absolutely nothing to do with–

Renee starts laughing or crying – it's impossible to tell which.

Vivienne Renee –

Renee I'm sorry.

Vivienne Are you alright?

Renee Sorry, sorry, I'm fine, I'm fine. (*Beat.*) A spin class? A spin class?! No, I'm sorry. Sorry. Just the image of me bouncing up and down on one of those bikes, sweatband round my head, it's just – Oh God! You have to laugh, don't you?

Vivienne You could do other things –

Renee Like what? Yoga? Aerobics? Meanwhile Anna's at home crying her eyes out because she's too tired to pick up a bloody hairbrush, and you want me to start fostering her independence via an hour of *Aqua Pilates* –

Vivienne Why not? (*Beat.*) It will give you time to yourself – give Anna the space that she needs. In this drive to keep her safe, Renee, you need to be careful you're not creating a situation in which she becomes completely dependent–

Renee Then maybe we should take a spin class together?

Beat.

Is Anna the oldest patient you see, Vivienne?

—

Do you have a *single* patient that is older than –

Vivienne I heard you.

Silence.

I know you're angry, Renee. I understand that you are feeling tired and frustrated and overwhelmed – but whatever it is that is causing that . . . It has very little to do with me.

———————

Anna I'm not wearing any make-up.

Oliver That's OK.

Anna I didn't have time to put any make-up on –

Oliver I've seen you without make-up –

Anna Noo, you haven't –

Oliver I slept next to you – like – loads of times –

Anna Still had it on, so . . .

Oliver You slept in your –

Anna Yeah.

    Beat.

Oliver You look really nice –

Anna (*disbelieving*) Yeah, OK –

Oliver No, I walked in here and I thought that – like, that was an actual thought I had – I'm not just saying that to . . . you know . . . I didn't walk in here and think, 'Shit, she doesn't have make-up on,' I just thought, 'I really like her face,' so . . .

    Beat.

Anna Thank you.

Oliver That's uh . . . that's OK.

    Silence.

/ I wanted to –

Anna Can I just – (*Beat.*) Sorry –

Oliver No, you go –

Anna Sorry, I just . . . my head's a bit – I'm worried I'll forget what I . . . what I want to say . . . if I don't –

Oliver It's fine. You first.

    Anna takes a deep breath, steadies herself.

Anna There's always been something wrong with me . . . my whole . . . my whole life they've told me there's something wrong with me, my whole life they've – 'don't do this' – 'don't do that' – but when you first met me you didn't know anything about me and you . . . you didn't think I was weird or crazy, you . . . you thought I was *brave* and . . . I've realised that if you can like me – if you could maybe – if you could – if you could love me? – if someone could love me who isn't like – biologically *programmed* to, then I . . . then I know I will get through this – I know I will have / a reason to –

Oliver Don't do that.

Beat.

Anna Don't do . . . don't do what?

Oliver Don't pressure me, don't . . . If I don't stay with you, then you'll . . . what? You'll hurt yourself?

Anna That's not what I was saying –

Oliver What were you saying then?

Anna I think I was . . . I think I was hoping that maybe you would – that it wouldn't be *pressure* – that maybe you would . . . *want* to be with me?

—

But I get it if you think this is all like . . . too much, or –

Oliver I don't care that you're ill.
Beat.
The first time you told me, it didn't make me want to run away or anything, it actually made me feel kind of . . . I dunno? . . . kind of special? You never tell anyone about it, but for whatever reason you decided to tell me and . . . and because you trusted me with this, um . . . this thing that embarrassed you, I thought it was OK to share something with you . . . something that embarrasses me?
So I took you to my place. I introduced you to my dad. And you used it to insult me, like . . . the first moment you got . . . you used that to make me feel like . . . like shit . . . and . . .

You know you haven't asked me a single question about myself? Two months we've been seeing each other – not a single one. And your mum keeps telling me that inside your head it's kind of . . . intense and . . . I know that's not your fault, but . . . I'm pretty sure being ill doesn't make you a horrible person, like, I'm pretty sure that's like . . . a choice, you know?

—

I just came over to do the right thing –

Anna The right thing –

Oliver In person. I wanted to wait a bit, wait until you were better before I told you, and you seem pretty great so –

Anna Sure, I'm great –

Oliver That's great –

Anna Listen, in the interests of self-improvement or or or whatever – if I hadn't – if I hadn't said those things to you . . . would you still want to be with me?

Oliver I don't know.
    Maybe.

    Pause.

Anna Cool. OK. See – it's good to learn these things about yourself – about life – all learning learning learning – I know I'll look back on this and go 'shouldn't have said that', 'shouldn't have said this' – but I can't, uh – I can't do that yet – I don't know how to – I don't know how to keep it all *inside* – like you can – I mean: you're standing there and I can't tell a single thing you're thinking or feeling and that is, uh . . . that is amazing – like if I could have any superpower, it wouldn't be superhuman strength or or or the ability to shoot lasers out of my eyeballs, it would be to stand across from you

107

right now and not give *anything* away, because how lucky are you, Oliver, how incredibly lucky are you, to be boring, / to be –

Oliver OK, I'm going –

Anna (*stepping in front of him*) What's your favourite colour?

   Beat.

Oliver Anna –

Anna Blue? Green?

Oliver I need to leave now –

Anna What type of music do you like? What makes you laugh? If you could eat only one food for the rest of your life what would it be?

Oliver Anna, stop it –

   She grips his face and tries to focus it on hers.

Anna Have you ever broken a leg or or or an arm? Has anyone ever betrayed you, Oliver? Has anyone ever hurt you? When was the last time you felt ashamed or or or embarrassed or –

Oliver What the fuck are you doing?

   He tries to disentangle himself, but Anna won't let go, she's hurting him.

Anna Tell me and I will keep it safe – I will protect it, I promise –

Oliver Get off me –

Anna We'll protect each other –

Oliver Ow, fucking –

Anna I won't tell anyone –

Oliver (*pushing her off*) GET OFF ME.

He stares at her, genuinely scared for the first time. She tries to move towards him and he raises his hands in defence.

DON'T – don't come near me – don't, um – don't call – don't – don't send your mother round to my *fucking* house – Just . . . just leave me alone, OK?

He moves past her and exits.
Anna tries to go after him, but comes back, disoriented – distressed. She scratches at her arms, her torso – the sensation of fabric on skin is intolerable so she takes off her jumper and throws it on the ground.
She struggles to breathe – panics – then:

Renee Just me, Anna. Have you had dinner yet?

She exits off to Anna's room.

Anna, are you asleep?

She walks back into the living room.

Anna?

She raises her head and registers the silence. Slowly, the panic sets in. She moves through the house calling Anna's name.

Anna!
Anna!
ANNA ANNA ANNA ANNA –

Anna steps out from her mother's bedroom.

Anna Yes?

She wears her mother's bathrobe. Despite this, there is something strangely majestic about the way she is dressed.

What? Why are you shouting?

Renee I couldn't find you.

Anna I was in your room.

Renee Why?

Anna Too messy in mine. Can't write in there.

Renee registers the pile of papers in Anna's hand.

Renee You're writing?

Anna grins. She is luminous.

Anna Since three o'clock this afternoon. One hundred and twenty-eight pages in and no sign of slowing down yet.

Renee That's, uh . . . that's incredible.

Anna It's not incredible, Mother.

Renee No?

Anna Wonderful, *maybe* – but not *incredible*.

Renee Sorry, that isn't what I –

Anna But you didn't, did you? You didn't say it was *wonderful*. You didn't say it was brilliant, or great, or tip-top-terrific, you didn't even say, 'Oh Anna, what a relief!' No, you chose the word *incredible*, which indicates there's some element of all this that defies logic or belief, when actually, there's a definite fucking reason for it, isn't there?

Beat.

Renee When did you stop?

Anna That's not important –

Renee When did you stop taking them, Anna?

Anna See – you're still talking about things as if they exist in total isolation, as if events can be understood without any consideration of the sequence leading up to them –

Renee takes out her mobile phone and dials Vivienne's number.

She won't talk to you.

I said: she won't talk to you. She's not my doctor any more, I have a new doctor now, Dr Bolton; they're sending me a letter.

Renee hangs up the phone.

I called her office, but Grace wouldn't put me through to her. Kept referring me back to the letter: I'm nineteen in two months. Standard procedure. That's all. And I'm racking my brain, trying to think what I could have done to make her go away, and then I ask: has my mum been to see her recently? And Grace didn't say anything – *couldn't* say anything – so she just . . . she thanked me for calling, and then she hung up.

Pause.

Renee Anna . . . I'm –

Anna Did you go to Oliver's house?

—

You've been doing a lot of visiting lately . . .

Renee I've been worried about you –

Anna Oh, it's fine. (*Beat.*) No – really! It's fine! Better than fine, kind of a relief, actually – Oliver's gone – Vivienne's gone – just a chance to start again, isn't it?

And the next available appointment with Dr Bolton is not until the 27th of June, which is still forty-five days away, so for forty-five days – through no fault of my own! – no one is supervising my medication, and I'm sure

Vivienne – if she was still my doctor – I'm sure Vivienne would be the first to tell you a patient isn't supposed to be medicating herself, so I thought it best I take a break for a while, and not like . . . a *long* break, but definitely longer than last time, because you can't try something once, watch it fail, and assume that's the end of the conversation, Mother. These things take time. These things take a *lot* of time – but now? *Now?*

It's happening, Mother – (*She taps her skull.*) I can *feel* it – the pathways are opening, chemical messages are being absorbed, and every word, every sentence, every chapter unfolds in real time, like opening a box within a box within a box within a box within a box within a box, always trusting, always knowing, always having complete confidence that one word will be followed by the next by the next by the next by the next by the next by the next – and Mother? – (*She indicates the papers in her hand.*) It's good. It's really good.

Pause.

Renee Well. I'm glad.

Anna Glad?

Renee Happy. I'm happy for you.

Anna Do you want to know what it's about?

Renee If you like.

Anna I can't tell you all of it.

Renee OK.

Anna I don't want to give it all away.

Renee I understand.

Anna But I can tell you it's about this girl called Meredith –

Renee Meredith?

Beat.

Anna Do you like the name Meredith?

Renee Um, I . . . I don't mind it, no?

Anna Good. Because I hated it at first: the only reason
I even considered using it was because it added an extra
layer of irony, but I looked it up and do you know what
it means? 'Magnificent'. Meredith means 'magnificent'.
It's an ancient Welsh word for a Great Lady, or a legendary
chief, it also means 'Protector of the Sea', and I'm not
entirely sure the significance of that yet, but there must be
something, must be something, I mean the whole world
was once an ocean, so that's a pretty phenomenal
mandate, don't you think? Nothing bigger than an ocean,
is there?

Renee No, I suppose there's / not –

Anna Exactly! Because Meredith is just, uh – (*She laughs.*)
She is just – (*She laughs.*) She is just fucking *brilliant*,
you know – the stuff of stars, and space, and those uh,
those uh, those uh, those clouds that gather round
mountaintops until everything *explodes*, and most of
the time it is . . . Oh God . . . most of the time it is
exhausting – but then there are moments like this one –
there are moments when everything seems to stop and
bend towards you – like the universe has scooped you up
and is carrying you inside of it – like it is telling you
things that are bigger than yourself – and Meredith's
mother – (*She laughs.*) Meredith's *mother* – (*She laughs.*)
Meredith's mother, she does not get this . . . *at all*, so she
buys these pills, right? Tries to make the girl take them,
but the girl's too smart, see? Hides them in the back of
her throat, spits them out as soon as she gets the chance,
so the mother grinds them down, crushes them into

113

powder, stirs it into the juice, sprinkles it on all the food –
(*Singing and sprinkling.*) Jingle Bells, Jingle Bells –
fucking Christmas meatballs, yeah? And this powder? It
blocks her all up, it cuts her off, it congeals across the
pathways of her brain until Meredith is slow and tired
and really not very interesting at all, and everyone keeps
leaving her, everyone keeps fucking leaving her, it's like
she has this total incapacity to hold on to anyone or
anything in her life that gives her even a microscopic
amount of joy, and I know that's a shit ending, I'm still
working on the ending, but the thing is, Mother, it's not
really a story at all, it's about *me*, I'm writing about *me*,
it's a memoir, yes, but also an exposé of sorts, and when
it's finished, when it's bound and wrapped and shipped
to all four corners of the known and visible world, I'm
going to take one copy and write on the inside cover:
'Dear Mother, I wrote this for you.'

   Beat.

I have to go now.

Renee Anna –

Anna I have to go, I have to go, I have to go –

Renee Where?

Anna Where are my keys, where are my fucking keys?

Renee You don't know how to drive.

Anna Then I'll walk.

Renee Where to?

Anna HarperCollins, or or or the one in the bubble.

Renee I'm sorry?

Anna You know, supercalifragilisticexpialidocious, bow
tie, bow tie, fucking stupid animal –

Renee Penguin.

Anna Yes! I'll go to Penguin! NO! HarperCollins. None of this paperback bullshit, would I be responsible for that, do you think?

Renee Responsible for what?

Anna The number of trees it takes to, whole forests maybe –

Renee Anna –

Anna Because I want it to be read, Mother, you know I do, but if it means I'm liable for any unnatural disturbance, then I just don't think –

Renee ANNA.

Anna What?

   Beat.

Renee I think you might need to slow down a bit, sweetheart.

Anna Slow down?

Renee Yes.

Anna Slow down?!

—

I don't think you understand how desperate this situation is, Mother. I don't think you understand – but of course *you* don't understand because you were never, you were *never* – and there are *millions,* do you understand *that*? There are millions of them out there right now, popping pills with their morning porridge or their Chocolate Shreddies, and soon they'll be adults, and some already are, and a good percentage of these half-baked fuckers know how to string a sentence together, and it only takes one, ONE, to write their story down, and then mine is just – I don't know – suggested reading –

scrollbar on Amazon – and then all of this work would be for nothing, and then I'll have to go back to, go back to – NO! – no no no no no –

She begins hitting her head, dropping all papers in the process.

STUPID STUPID STUPID STUPID STUPID.

She sobs, then wails, rubs her wrists on her body as if erasing some kind of physical pain, then stops and wipes the snot from her face.

Fuck 'em, they're not me, right?

She gathers the papers together.

I am the Chief. I am the Great Lady. I am the Protector of the FUCKING sea, because I see things, you know? Oh, I see them alright, and they are slow and they are tired and they are rooted to the ground, but I have been released! I am set free! (*Tapping the pages.*) I have been delivered to create a record of my experiences – and you might not believe me, you may deny me for what I truly am and what I always was, but my father . . . my father . . . (*Beat. She searches frantically through her pages.*) My my my my my my my my . . . (*Finding her place, then reading:*) 'My father would come home from work, pick me up and stand me on the kitchen table. "Read me a story," he'd say, and even though he was the only person in the room, he would move as far away from me as possible and pretend he was in a crowd of thousands: "Louder, Anna . . . no one can hear you up the back . . . "'

Beat.

I have to go now, Mother.

Renee (*carefully; edging closer to her*) Anna –

Anna I'm sorry, Mother, I really do have to go now –

Renee (*almost upon her*) Anna . . . *please* . . . listen to me, sweetheart . . . I need you to –

    Anna bolts.
      She runs past her mother and escapes the house.
      Everything is fast-moving, heightened, and abundantly clear: Anna is experiencing a revelation – one she's desperate to share.
      And then it gets a little scarier and a little louder, and things stop making so much sense.
      Several seconds of maximum energy and then –

A long silence.

Renee She said she couldn't make it.

—

    Too many appointments.

—

    And yes, I did ask her. I know you think I didn't, but I did.

—

    Try not to take it personally, OK? They share the same office – she and Dr Bolton – so they must talk. You can't share the same office and not talk.

—

    How is he?

—

    Vivienne said he's good, one of the best, so that's . . . that's something.

—

    (*Indicating the room.*) It's not too bad, is it? Nice big desk. Bed. Sink. Lovely window.

—

    Would you like to go for a walk? You could show me around?

—

Isabel called. She asked you to call her back, but I wasn't sure if you'd be able to, or if you'd want to, so I told her you'd gone away for a while, and then she asked where, so I said you'd gone overseas, and then she asked where overseas, and I said: 'Jesus Christ, Izzy, maybe if you were a better fucking friend you'd know.'

—

I didn't say that last part.

—

I thought it though.

—

Would you like to go overseas? We can, if you want to. There doesn't have to be reason. We should go somewhere – someplace we've never been before – would you like that?

—

I've started seeing someone, actually. A doctor. Not in the romantic sense, unfortunately, though that would be nice. He's a bit young for me anyway, so . . .

—

He thinks I have depression – may have had – for quite a while –

Anna What do you want me to say to that?

Beat.

Renee I was hoping you might let me talk, and perhaps, perhaps you could listen and –

Anna What happened to my pages?

Renee Don't change the subject.

Anna What did you do with them?

Renee Anna –

Anna Do you still have them? Have you thrown them out?

Renee My doctor suggested I talk to you about some of my own issues in the hope that we might reach some kind of mutual –

Anna I hate you.
—

I do. I mean that. I knew we were different, but this is just . . . I worked so hard on that, and it was good, I know it was good –

Renee It was beautiful.
—

You're a good writer, Anna.
—

Anna That's it?
Are you kidding me? That's all you're going to say?

Renee Yes.

Anna There's nothing else?

Renee No.

Anna But I can see it, hovering underneath that vein of yours, that big one, right there, lightning rod across your forehead, come on, Mum, say it, say it quick, say it before it *explodes*.

Silence.
Renee reaches into her bag and pulls out Anna's pages, now delicately filed and bound.

Renee I couldn't find them all.
You dropped most of it in the street, put the rest through people's letterboxes – I had to go round to each of the neighbours and ask for them back, which meant I had to talk to them, and I've been putting that off since we moved here . . . oh, I don't know? . . . fifteen years ago and . . .
I'm sorry. I shouldn't joke about that.

She places the pages near Anna.

I think they're mostly in the right order now.

Silence.

You know, it still astounds me that I could create someone with such . . . capacity . . . for feeling . . . who has the skill to translate that into words, and then the commitment to see that through not one page, but hundreds. I could never do something like that – your father, maybe him, yes – but not me.

—

I imagine there are certain . . . changes . . . that need to happen, to turn real lives, *our* lives, into a story. And I didn't mind that so much – really, I didn't. I could forgive the mild inaccuracies, the differences that occur in that giant leap between recollections, and I do understand the need to tell your story, your way, for you . . . But to just *assume* that someone else's doesn't exist? To just assume that you know all there is to know about a person, having never once asked, or questioned, to then write that person with all the complexity of a fairy-tale witch, despite the fact that she has been here, has always been here, this living archive of everything you have ever experienced . . .

She pauses, calms herself.

Have I ever done anything right by you?
    Think of something. Please.
    I need you to tell me one thing I have done that wasn't completely out of order.

Silence.
    Renee collects her things.

Anna Where are you going?

Renee Home.

Anna It's two hours back.

Renee I'm tired.

Anna You only just got here.

Renee And now I'm going home.

Anna You can nap on my bed if you want.

Renee I've got my own to get back to.

Anna Just for a bit.

Renee You don't even want me here.

Anna No, I do –

Renee No, no, you said to me, over the phone: 'I don't want you here.'

Anna I don't have anyone else.

Renee Anna –

Anna I don't.

Renee That's not going to work on me any more –

Anna I'm not saying it to make you feel sorry for me. It's the truth.

Silence.

Renee Five more minutes.

She slips her shoes off and sits on the bed.

Sorry if the feet smell.

Anna That's OK.

Renee You might want to sit up here where the air is clearer.

Anna It's fine.

Renee I can smell them from here –

Anna It really doesn't matter, Mum.

Renee settles in. A few moments of silence.

Anna Was Dad the only person you ever loved?

Renee Where did that come from?

Anna I don't know.
Was he though?

Renee No.

Anna So you had boyfriends before Dad?

Renee I wasn't some sexless android before I met your father.

Anna How many people have you had sex with?

Renee Anna!

Anna Are you uncomfortable speaking about this?

Renee A little.

Anna Why?

Renee I thought I was supposed to be having a nap.

Anna Why are you uncomfortable?

Renee Well, it's not like asking me what I had for breakfast, is it?

Anna I'm trying, Mum.

Renee So you start with this?!

Anna shrugs.

A few.

Anna How many's a few?

Renee A lady never tells.

Anna Why not?

Renee Sorry?

Anna Why can't the lady ever tell?

Renee Oh I don't know, it's all about reputation, isn't it?

Anna Maybe in 1959 –

Renee Seven. (*Beat.*) Seven and a half. I slept with seven and a half people before your father.

Anna Who's the half?

Renee Tracy Evans. Didn't do much for either of us so we stopped and made avocado face masks instead.
  How many have you slept with?

Anna Do you really want to know?

Renee No. How many have you slept with?

Anna Double yours.

  Beat.

Renee How did you even have the time?!

Anna It's dating that takes up all the time; sex is over in seven minutes or less.
  Too much?

Renee No.

Anna You're judging me.

Renee I'm not.

Anna Your daughter's a tramp.

Renee My daughter is wonderful. I just don't expect anyone else to realise that in seven minutes or less.

Anna Yeah, well . . . no one in here is going to have sex with me, so . . .

Renee No boys around?

Anna They're *around* . . . I just don't want them to see me while I'm covered in fur.

She pulls up her trouser leg.

Renee It's really not that bad.

Anna It's disgusting.

Renee digs around in her bag. She hands Anna a pack of disposable razors.

Renee I picked these up on the way in. I'm not leaving them here with you. And I'm not supporting any funny business, OK? I want you coming home with a clear state of mind not a severe case of crabs; do you understand me?

She busies herself around the room.

Do you have a bowl of some kind? For the water? There's shaving cream in my bag too.

Anna finds it and takes it out.

Anna Do you want to?

Renee Sorry?

Anna I won't get in trouble that way. If anyone walks in, you can say I never touched it and it wouldn't be a lie. (*Beat.*) If that's weird, if you think that's weird –

Renee It's not weird.

Anna Are you sure?

Renee Where should we . . .

Anna sits down, and after a bit of clumsy adjustment, places her legs across her mother's lap. Renee begins to apply the shaving cream.

Is this OK? Not too cold?

Anna shakes her head.

No sudden movements, alright?

Renee begins, gentle delicate strokes. She does this for some time, and then:

Anna I'm eight years old, we have guests and my hand is in the ice bucket. But it's not working. I can feel myself disappearing. I'm half here, half not, and it's ridiculous – I know it's ridiculous – how could someone be here, and yet not be here? – but I don't know how to explain it to you: that I need to put my hand in the ice because the sensation reminds me I'm still connected to the earth – and I don't want to embarrass you in front of your guests – so when you ask what I'm doing, I just cry and say what I hope is more acceptable: 'I don't know where I am.'

And you come up to me, you take my hand out of the bucket, you warm it up between your own hands, and you say: 'Anna, you're with me.' And the logic of that was just so . . . *faultless* . . . how could I argue with it?

Of course. Yes. That's exactly where I am. I'm with you.

Renee continues.
The lights slowly fade to black.

End of play.